BUT ENCOURAGE ONE ANOTHER DAILY
AS LONG AS IT IS CALLED TODAY

Titles in the Seedbed Daily Text series:

he
eedbed
aily Text

BUT ENCOURAGE ONE ANOTHER DAILY
AS LONG AS IT IS CALLED TODAY

ouragement

. WALT

Unless otherwise noted, Scripture quotations are taken from the Holy Bible, New International Version®, NIV® Copyright © 1973, 1978, 1984, 2011 by Biblica, Inc.™ Used by permission of Zondervan. All rights reserved worldwide. www.zondervan.com The "NIV" and "New International Version" are trademarks registered in the United States Patent and Trademark Office by Biblica, Inc.™ All rights reserved worldwide.

Scripture quotations marked NASB are taken from the New American Standard Bible® (NASB), Copyright © 1960, 1962, 1963, 1968, 1971, 1972, 1973, 1975, 1977, 1995 by The Lockman Foundation. Used by permission. www.Lockman.org.

Scripture quotations marked ESV are from the ESV® Bible (The Holy Bible, English Standard Version®), copyright © 2001 by Crossway, a publishing ministry of Good News Publishers. Used by permission. All rights reserved.

Printed in the United States of America

Cover and page design by Strange Last Name
Typesetting by PerfecType, Nashville, Tennessee

Walt, J. D. (John David)
   But encourage one another daily, as long as it is called today : encouragement / J.D. Walt. – Franklin, Tennessee : Seedbed Publishing, ©2022.

      pages ; cm. . – (Seedbed daily text)

      Includes bibliographical references.
      ISBN: 9781628249538 (paperback)
      ISBN: 9781628249545 (mobi)
      ISBN: 9781628249552 (epub)
      ISBN: 9781628249569 (pdf)
      OCLC: 1310402462

      1. Encouragement--Religious aspects--Christianity. 2. Courage--Religious aspects--Christianity. I. Title. II. Series. III. Encouragement.

BV4647.E53 W36 2022   242   2022936064

SEEDBED PUBLISHING
Franklin, Tennessee
seedbed.com

Contents

An Invitation to Awakening

This resource comes with an invitation.

The invitation is as simple as it is comprehensive. It is not an invitation to commit your life to this or that cause or to join an organization or to purchase another book. The invitation is this: to wake up to the life you always hoped was possible and the reason you were put on planet Earth.

It begins with following Jesus Christ. In case you are unaware, Jesus was born in the first century BCE into a poor family from Nazareth, a small village located in what is modern-day Israel. While his birth was associated with extraordinary phenomena, we know little about his childhood. At approximately thirty years of age, Jesus began a public mission of preaching, teaching, and healing throughout the region known as Galilee. His mission was characterized by miraculous signs and wonders; extravagant care of the poor and marginalized; and multiple unconventional claims about his own identity and purpose. In short, he claimed to be the incarnate Son of God with the mission and power to save people from sin, deliver them from death, and bring them into the now and eternal kingdom of God—on earth as it is in heaven.

In the spring of his thirty-third year, during the Jewish Passover celebration, Jesus was arrested by the religious authorities, put on trial in the middle of the night, and at their urging, sentenced to death by a Roman governor. On the day known to history as Good Friday, Jesus was crucified on a Roman cross. He was buried in a borrowed tomb. On the following Sunday, according to multiple eyewitness accounts, he was physically raised from the dead. He appeared to hundreds of people, taught his disciples, and prepared for what was to come.

Forty days after the resurrection, Jesus ascended bodily into the heavens where, according to the Bible, he sits at the right hand of God, as the Lord of heaven and earth. Ten days after his ascension, in a gathering of 120 people on the day of Pentecost, a Jewish day of celebration, something truly extraordinary happened. A loud and powerful wind swept over the people gathered. Pillars of what appeared to be fire descended upon the followers of Jesus. The Holy Spirit, the presence and power of God, filled the people, and the church was born. After this, the followers of Jesus went forth and began to do the very things Jesus did—preaching, teaching, and healing—planting churches and making disciples all over the world. Today, more than two thousand years later, the movement has reached us. This is the Great Awakening, and it has never stopped.

Yes, two thousand years hence and more than two billion followers of Jesus later, this awakening movement of Jesus Christ and his church stands stronger than ever. Billions of ordinary people the world over have discovered in Jesus Christ an awakened life they never imagined possible. They have overcome challenges, defeated addictions, endured untenable hardships and suffering with unexplainable joy, and stared death in the face with the joyful confidence of eternal life. They have healed the sick, gathered the outcasts, embraced the oppressed, loved the poor, contended for justice, labored for peace, cared for the dying, and, yes, even raised the dead.

We all face many challenges and problems. They are deeply personal, yet when joined together, they create enormous and complex chaos in the world, from our hearts to our homes to our churches and our cities. All of this chaos traces to two originating problems: sin and death. Sin, far beyond mere moral failure, describes the fundamental broken condition of every human being. Sin separates us from God and others, distorts and destroys our deepest identity as the image-bearers of God, and poses a fatal problem from which we cannot save ourselves. It results in an ever-diminishing quality of life and ultimately ends in eternal death. Because Jesus lived a life of sinless perfection, he is able to save us from sin and restore us to a right relationship with God, others, and ourselves. He did this through his sacrificial death on the cross on our behalf. Because Jesus rose from the dead, he is able to deliver us from death and bring us into a quality of life both eternal and unending.

This is the gospel of Jesus Christ: pardon from the penalty of sin, freedom from the power of sin, deliverance from the grip of death, and awakening to the supernatural empowerment of the Holy Spirit to live powerfully for the good of others and the glory of God. Jesus asks only that we acknowledge our broken selves as failed sinners, trust him as our Savior, and follow him as our Lord. Following Jesus does not mean an easy life; however, it does lead to a life of power and purpose, joy in the face of suffering, and profound, even world-changing, love for God and people.

All of this is admittedly a lot to take in. Remember, this is an invitation. Will you follow Jesus? Don't let the failings of his followers deter you. Come and see for yourself.

Here's a prayer to get you started:

> Our Father in heaven, it's me (say your name). I want to know you. I want to live an awakened life. I confess I am a sinner. I have failed myself, others, and you in many ways. I know you made me for a purpose, and I want to fulfill that purpose with my one life. I want to follow Jesus Christ. Jesus, thank you for the gift of your life and death and resurrection and ascension on my behalf. I want to walk in relationship with you as Savior and Lord. Would you lead me into the fullness and newness of life I was made for? I am ready to follow you. Come, Holy Spirit, and fill me with the love, power, and purposes of God. I pray these things by faith in the name of Jesus, amen.

It would be our privilege to help you get started and grow deeper in this awakened life of following Jesus. For some next steps and encouragements, visit seedbed.com/awaken.

How the Daily Text Works

It seems obvious to say, but the Daily Text is written every day. Mostly it is written the day before it is scheduled to release online.

Before you read further, you are cordially invited to subscribe to and receive the daily e-mail. Visit seedbed.com /dailytext to get started. Also, check out the popular Facebook group, Seedbed Daily Text.

Eventually, the daily postings become part of a Daily Text discipleship resource. That's what you hold in your hands now.

It's not exactly a Bible study, though the Bible is both the source and subject. You will learn something about the Bible along the way: its history, context, original languages, and authors. The goal is not educational in nature, but transformational. Seedbed is more interested in folks knowing Jesus than knowing *about* Jesus.

To that end, each reading begins with the definitive inspiration of the Holy Spirit, the ongoing, unfolding text of Scripture. Following that is a short and, hopefully, substantive insight from the text and some aspect of its meaning. For insight to lead to deeper influence, we turn the text into prayer. Finally, influence must run its course toward impact. This is why we ask each other questions. These questions are not designed to elicit information but to crystallize intention.

Discipleship always leads from inspiration to intention and from attention to action.

Using the Daily Text as a Discipleship Curricular Resource for Groups

While Scripture always addresses us personally, it is not written to us individually. The content of Scripture cries out for a community to address. The Daily Text is made for discipleship in community. This resource can work in several different ways. It could be read like a traditional book, a few pages or chapters at a time. Though unadvisable, the readings could be crammed in on the night before the meeting. Keep in mind, the Daily Text is not called the Daily Text for kicks. We believe Scripture is worthy of our most focused and consistent attention. Every day. We all have misses, but let's make every day more than a noble aspiration. Let's make it our covenant with one another.

For Use with Bands

In our judgment, the best and highest use of the Daily Text is made through what we call banded discipleship. A band is a same-gender group of three to five people who read together, pray together, and meet together to become the love of God for one another and the world. With banded discipleship, the daily readings serve more as a common text for the band and grist for the interpersonal conversation mill between meetings. The band meeting is reserved for the specialized activities of high-bar discipleship.

To learn more about bands and banded discipleship, visit discipleshipbands.com. Be sure to download the free *Discipleship Bands: A Practical Field Guide* or order a supply of the printed booklets online. Also be sure to explore Discipleship Bands, our native app designed specifically for the practice of banded discipleship, in the App Store or Google Play.

For Use with Classes and Small Groups

The Daily Text has also proven to be a helpful discipleship resource for a variety of small groups, from community groups to Sunday school classes. Here are some suggested guidelines for deploying the Daily Text as a resource for a small group or class setting:

1. Hearing the Text

Invite the group to settle into silence for a period of no less than one and no more than five minutes. Ask an appointed person to keep time and to read the biblical text covering the period of days since the last group meeting. Allow at least one minute of silence following the reading of the text.

2. Responding to the Text

Invite anyone from the group to respond to the reading by answering these prompts: What did you hear? What did you see? What did you otherwise sense from the Lord?

3. Sharing Insights and Implications for Discipleship

Moving in an orderly rotation (or free-for-all), invite people to share insights and implications from the week's readings.

What did you find challenging, encouraging, provocative, comforting, invasive, inspiring, corrective, affirming, guiding, or warning? Allow group conversation to proceed at will. Limit to one sharing item per turn, with multiple rounds of discussion.

4. Shaping Intentions for Prayer

Invite each person in the group to share a single discipleship intention for the week ahead. It is helpful if the intention can also be framed as a question the group can use to check in from the prior week. At each person's turn, he or she is invited to share how their intention went during the previous week. The class or group can open and close their meeting according to their established patterns.

BUT ENCOURAGE ONE ANOTHER DAILY

AS LONG AS IT IS CALLED TODAY

Encourage One Another Daily, As Long As It Is Called "Today"

HEBREWS 3:13 | But encourage one another daily, as long as it is called "Today," so that none of you may be hardened by sin's deceitfulness.

Consider This

For the next fifty-nine days we are going to be digging a deep well of encouragement. We will delve into what the Holy Spirit has revealed to us about the practice and ministry of encouragement: how it works, how to do it, and so forth. In the process, we will "encourage one another daily, as long as it is called 'Today,' so that none of [us] may be hardened by sin's deceitfulness."

I have become convinced that the greatest and most singular need people who want to wake up, follow Jesus, and become imbued with his supernatural presence and power in the everyday world—which is holy love—is courage. We need to have courage put into us. And we need it not just every now and then or before a big challenge or in the midst of a hard struggle or loss. So how often do we need to be encouraged?

But encourage one another daily, as long as it is called "Today," . . .

Every. Single. Day.

A couple of years ago I created an acronym for the things I want to sow into my own life every single day in order to be more deeply whole in my physical body and alive in Christ by the power of the Spirit. The acronym is SEEDS.

S = Sunshine and Scripture (outside and inside)

E = Exercise (just do something because anything is better than nothing)

E = Encouragement (give and receive)

D = Diet (fasted lifestyle with feasting rhythms)

S = Sleep and Spirit (passive and active)

One of these things is not quite like the others: encouragement. We all understand encouragement at a certain level. It's the William Wallace speech to his fear-filled warriors in *Braveheart*. It's Knute Rockne to the Fighting Irish in the Notre Dame locker room. On we could go. But encouragement, as the Bible reveals, is of another quality and order of magnitude. Here is my working definition:

> To encourage in the biblical sense of the term is to stand in the stead and agency of Jesus, participating in the work of the Holy Spirit, to minister grace to human beings at the level of their inner person, communicating, conveying, and imparting life, love, courage, comfort, consolation, joy, peace, hope, faith, and other dispensations and manifestations of the kingdom of heaven as the moment invites or requires.

But encourage one another daily, as long as it is called "Today," . . .

As you can see, we are going in deep. This awakening practice of encouragement will change the character of your heart and the climate of your home. In fact, if you can get even a handful from your local church to join in with this kind of sowing work, it will change the culture of your community into one of encouragement, and if this gets loose in a small town or city—oh my! This work of encouragement comprises the core essence and ethos of what we call "banded discipleship."

The Prayer

God our Father, you are the God of all encouragement. Thank you for your Son, Jesus, who is the ultimate exemplar of both courage and encouragement. No one has encouraged the human race more than Jesus Christ of Nazareth, crucified and risen from the dead, ascended to your right hand, where he ever lives to encourage the saints. Come, Holy Spirit, teach and train us as agents of encouragement. It seems simple enough, and yet we know there is an art and craft and skill to anything your Spirit does through human agency. Come and encourage us that we might encourage others. We pray in Jesus' name, amen.

The Questions

- Can you remember the last time someone deeply encouraged you? How about when you last deeply encouraged another? What do you remember about these occasions?

2 | Getting Beyond Our Bumper Sticker Theology

HEBREWS 3:13 | But <u>encourage one another daily, as long as it is called "Today," so that none of you may be hardened by sin's deceitfulness.</u>

Consider This

But encourage one another daily, as long as it is called "Today," . . .

It's tempting and would be easy to rip this text out of its context and interpret it through the lens of our time, allowing our own cultural mix of stories, fables, heroes, and folklore (a.k.a. movies) to tell us what encouragement really means.

I can already see the refrigerator magnet: "Encourage One Another Daily." Or the bumper sticker: "Encourage One Another Today."

Upon seeing it we would hasten to pat someone on the back, tell them they could do it, or commend the waiter for doing a good job and feel like we had done it. And while there is always ample need for kind words and thoughtful gestures, let's not confuse them for what the Bible is talking about in this verse.

Did you see what I did with the refrigerator magnets? I left out what may be the most significant word in the verse. Did you see it? It's the first word: *but.*

Conjunction junction, what's your function? There is a strategically placed word here. It tells us that this admonition to "encourage one another daily, as long as it is called 'Today'" is in contrast to something that has gone before. It calls us to explore the context. As my New Testament ninja Bible teacher Dr. Ben Witherington III fondly says, "A text without a context is merely a pretext for your own text." If you have read previous Daily Text series, you know this is a no-fluff-zone when it comes to the biblical text. We are learning to read well together.

The context here is fascinating, and we will take a day or two to explore it in some depth as it will reveal significant layers of nuanced meaning for us. Let's look back to verse 12: "See to it, brothers and sisters, that none of you has a sinful, unbelieving heart that turns away from the living God."

We must encourage one another daily as long as it is called "today" not because we all need more attaboys and pats on the back. It's way more serious than that. This cuts to the very core of the human condition. The nature of fallen, broken human beings can be diagnosed as follows: "a sinful, unbelieving heart that turns away from the living God." Though we have been saved from the penalty of sin by the life, death, resurrection, and ascension of Jesus Christ, sin still crouches at the door.

And we aren't talking about mere bad behavior here and the temptation to have a second piece of Aunt Myrtle's coconut cream pie. Behavior is a symptom. Sin is the disease. We need a far more robust understanding of what sin is and how sin works if we are to truly understand what grace is and how salvation works. Our typical view of sin and salvation is very transactional, and though there is definitely a forensic dimension to sin, it is far more complex and sophisticated than that. Verse 12 gives us perhaps the most succinct definition of what sin most deeply is: an "unbelieving heart that turns away from the living God." This is why encouragement is so essential. Hear the text now with the context: "See to it, brothers and sisters, that none of you has a sinful, unbelieving heart that turns away from the living God. But encourage one another daily, as long as it is called 'Today.'"

Finally, you have undoubtedly noticed what else got cut out of our refrigerator magnet and bumper sticker versions—the whole second half of verse 13: "so that none of you may be hardened by sin's deceitfulness."

The human heart is so easily deceived, and sin (a.k.a. an "unbelieving heart") is unbelievably deceitful. Behavior management is not the cure for sin's deceitfulness. That is like taking cough syrup for lung cancer. The ongoing Holy Spirit chemotherapy for the deceitful sin cancer of an unbelieving heart is thick encouragement.

The Prayer

God our Father, forgive us for our flat and thin ways of engaging the revelation of your Word. Jesus, as the Word made flesh, would you be our teacher, causing our hearts to burn as you unfold the Scriptures, the very heart and now wisdom of eternal life? Just as your Spirit inspired the Word, may the Spirit now interpret it to our inmost beings that it might work itself into every conceivable expression of our lives, for our good, for others' gain, for your glory. In Jesus' name, amen.

The Questions

- How are you resonating with the connection being made between the nature of sin and the call for encouragement? Will you help dig this well, or would you rather go back to the bumper sticker?

The Most Dangerous Place on Earth

3

HEBREWS 3:12–13 | See to it, brothers and sisters, that none of you has a sinful, unbelieving heart that turns away from the living God. But encourage one another daily, as long as it is called "Today," so that none of you may be hardened by sin's deceitfulness.

Consider This

It's a beautiful and powerful thing when Scripture quotes Scripture. In fact, the only way to understand Scripture is through a wider and deeper Holy Spirit–inspired reading of

Scripture. I want you to notice how the Bible regularly does this. This word, "encourage one another daily," can be read at face value, and yet there is a much deeper context we must explore to get at what it means. If we back up yet a few more verses, we see the text quoted from Psalm 95:

> So, as the Holy Spirit says:
>
> "Today, if you hear his voice,
>   do not harden your hearts
> as you did in the rebellion,
>   during the time of testing in the wilderness,
> where your ancestors tested and tried me,
>   though for forty years they saw what I did.
> That is why I was angry with that generation;
>   I said, 'Their hearts are always going astray,
>   and they have not known my ways.'
> So I declared on oath in my anger,
>   'They shall never enter my rest.'" (Heb. 3:7–11)

So the writer of Hebrews is remembering Psalm 95, which is remembering the story of Meribah, which is the occasion in the wilderness when the people were facing a crisis of a lack of water. Rather than leaning into the God who had provided for them every step of the way, they began to quarrel bitterly among themselves and grumble harshly against their leaders. It was a defining moment, a place where their faith was tested and where their faith failed. It turned out to be the place where their hearts began to be hardened.

Now, in light of this context, read our text yet again:

See to it, brothers and sisters, that none of you has a sinful, unbelieving heart that turns away from the living God. But encourage one another daily, as long as it is called "Today," so that none of you may be hardened by sin's deceitfulness.

Over the course of our lives, all of us have been through difficult trials. Unjust treatment, unforeseen losses, tragic deaths, life-stealing diseases, betrayals, relationship failures, and all manner of pain and suffering. These things create wilderness seasons that can go on for long periods of time. These are the places where we slowly and often imperceptibly lose faith in God. We would rarely identify it as such, but we begin to shrink back from real trust. We believe in principle but not in an everyday kind of trusting reality. We take on a wilderness wound, and our hearts slowly begin to harden. We don't so much choose hardness as we fail to pursue healing. We allow a wall of protection to be constructed around our heart, and while it does protect us in some ways, it also slowly and imperceptibly isolates us from God and others.

This is how sin deceives us. We mistakenly focus on sin at the level of our behaviors, but our behaviors are merely the symptoms of the sickness. Sin, in its deepest essence, is the condition of an unbelieving heart, and an unbelieving or untrusting heart inevitably becomes a hardened heart. And a hardened heart is the most dangerous place on earth.

So what does encouragement have to do with any of this? Psalm 95 says, "Today, if only you would hear his voice" (v. 7).

Encouragement, in the biblical sense of the term, is about personally and particularly hearing the voice of God from another person. As we encourage one another, we learn to speak to one another in the voice of God in the humble authority of Jesus in the loving power of the Holy Spirit. This doesn't come to us naturally. It only comes supernaturally, and yet it is a learned way.

As long as it is called "Today," . . .

The Prayer

God our Father, we want to pray with the psalmist today, "Search me, God, and know my heart; test me and know my anxious thoughts. See if there is any offensive way in me, and lead me in the way everlasting" (Ps. 139:23–24). Lord Jesus, we open our hearts to the searching, searing, and saving light of your Word and Holy Spirit. Are our hearts hardened? We wait before you in humility. Speak, Lord. Your sons and daughters are listening. We want to hear your voice. In Jesus' name, amen.

The Questions

- Are you aware that your heart could be hardened and you could have no idea of it? How does that affect you? What does it make you want to do? How does it make you want to respond?

On the Difference between Believing in God and Believing God

4

HEBREWS 3:12–13 | See to it, brothers and sisters, that none of you has a sinful, unbelieving heart that turns away from the living God. But encourage one another daily, as long as it is called "Today," so that none of you may be hardened by sin's deceitfulness.

Consider This

See to it, brothers and sisters, that none of you has a sinful, unbelieving heart that turns away from the living God.

It is easy to read this and think, "Of course I believe in God." An unbelieving heart is a far more subtle thing, and it can be hard to see it coming. The assault of darkness, evil, and even suffering and hardship is not to get us to stop believing *in* God. It is to cause us to stop *believing* God. You see the difference, don't you? It is an easy thing to believe in God. It is another thing entirely to believe God. The former is an affirmation of faith. The latter is faith itself. There are many souls who believe in God, and yet their hearts have turned away from the living God. I am writing this series as a response to the admonition in today's text: "See to it." This is what I would call flagrant encouragement.

We are living in a wilderness of sin, and by "we" I mean Christians who are living in the United States of America.

Our hearts have become hardened by sin's deceitfulness. COVID-19 has not caused this situation. It has only revealed it to us, and it has in all likelihood accelerated this hardening of hearts. Already, as many read this, tension is rising up within, which is itself a sign of both a defensiveness and an offensiveness—both of which are signs of a warring spirit—which is the nature of the reactiveness of a hardened heart. Over the past fifty years, this nation has become slowly ravaged by an increasingly toxic, partisan battle of political ideologies, which have infiltrated the body of Christ and become almost inextricably intertwined and wrapped in thin and often dubious biblical and theological justifications and warrants for our politically partisan positions and convictions.

To be clear, Jesus Christ is always political—never partisan. The single most explosive political statement ever made from the first century to the twenty-first century is this one: Jesus Christ is Lord. It is an affront and direct assault on the kingdoms of this world (even these United States). And while it is the most threatening declaration to the kingdoms of the world, it is also the most nonpartisan declaration. Every party should find it equally offensive. The belief that any political party aligns with the lordship of Jesus Christ is the ultimate deception and the most dangerous alliance of all.

From the earliest days of the Old Testament to the present day, the people of God have made all manner of alliances with other nations, political leaders, parties, and causes in order to promote and protect their interests and preferred vision. "Jesus Christ is Lord" is a fiercely political statement because it effectively means no other alliances.

When biblical/theological truth becomes tainted and compromised by ideological frameworks and pragmatic alliances, it leads invariably to idolatry. An idol is anything or anyone we put our hope in other than or in addition to Jesus Christ. Idols are lifeless things that promise flourishing life, and when we put our hope in a lifeless thing in pursuit of a flourishing life, we become lifeless. It's why the tell-tale sign of idolatry is hard-heartedness. There is only one response to hard-heartedness—confession and repentance. Tragically, the person with a hard heart is all too often the last one to know.

So what am I saying in this super-sticky place I recognize I am getting myself into? I am saying a lot of things, and I am not saying a lot of other things. It is too much to sort out in such a short place. My considered opinion is the people of God in our time are seriously compromised by the party spirit, deeply asleep, and hardened in heart. Could your heart be hardened by sin's deceitfulness? Will you open your heart and mind to the searchlight of the Holy Spirit? Would you step onto the threshing floor of God's mercy and allow yourself to be winnowed by Jesus Christ himself?

We have all been through a cataclysm that has put our hearts in perilous places. It is entirely possible that we have hardened our hearts slowly and imperceptibly over the course of these long months. It has brought bitter conflict, quarreling, and grumbling into our hearts, homes, churches, and cities. We must reckon with this if we are to be set free from it and be healed.

The Prayer

God our Father, we want to humble ourselves and confess and repent of the deceitfulness of sin. We want to acknowledge that our hearts are susceptible to being deceived. Would you pour out your grace and mercy on us in such a way that it leads to deep self-knowledge and humble honesty? Where have we turned on other people? Where do we no longer give the benefit of the doubt? Where are we making human beings into mortal enemies? Where have we made alliances with ungodly idols in order to attempt to effect godly things? Where have we gotten it wrong? Come, Holy Spirit, awaken our spirits and soften our hearts. In Jesus' name, amen.

The Question

- How do you see the difference between believing in God and believing God?

5 The Journey from Me to We and Why It Matters

JUDGES 6:11–12 | The angel of the LORD came and sat down under the oak in Ophrah that belonged to Joash the Abiezrite, where his son Gideon was threshing wheat in a winepress to keep it from the Midianites. When the angel of the Lord appeared to Gideon, he said, "The Lord is with you, mighty warrior."

Consider This

Today we come to a beautiful example of biblical encouragement.

Let's set the stage. We are in the period of the judges. The people of God are in the promised land, and yet they are under oppression. One step forward, ten steps back is always par for the course when following God. The unholy trifecta of darkness—the world, the flesh, and the Devil— always comes against the movement of God. Sometimes it is spiritual warfare. Sometimes it comes as a result of God's people phoning it in. In this case it is the latter. Judges 6 opens with this word: "The Israelites did evil in the eyes of the Lord, and for seven years he gave them into the hands of the Midianites" (v. 1).

It was really bad. How bad was it? Thanks for asking. We thought COVID-19 was bad. Get a load of this:

> Because the power of Midian was so oppressive, the Israelites prepared shelters for themselves in mountain clefts, caves and strongholds. Whenever the Israelites planted their crops, the Midianites, Amalekites and other eastern peoples invaded the country. They camped on the land and ruined the crops all the way to Gaza and did not spare a living thing for Israel, neither sheep nor cattle nor donkeys. They came up with their

> livestock and their tents like swarms of locusts. It was impossible to count them or their camels; they invaded the land to ravage it. (Judg. 6:2–5)

There is only one upside of this kind of suffering and hardship—desperation. Here's the pivot: "Midian so impoverished the Israelites that they cried out to the LORD for help" (Judg. 6:6).

Rescue always begins with remembering the story as revealed by the Word of God. To remember is to re-attach to. Get it? Re-member.

> When the Israelites cried out to the LORD because of Midian, he sent them a prophet, who said, "This is what the LORD, the God of Israel, says: I brought you up out of Egypt, out of the land of slavery. I rescued you from the hand of the Egyptians. And I delivered you from the hand of all your oppressors; I drove them out before you and gave you their land. I said to you, 'I am the LORD your God; do not worship the gods of the Amorites, in whose land you live.' But you have not listened to me." (Judg. 6:7–10)

No one alive had ever lived in Egypt as a slave or been present at the Red Sea. Yet this was not history for them. It was their right here, right now story. Biblical encouragement requires a kind of remembering beyond mere historical memory. Look at how the prophet-encourager works here: I brought *you* up out of Egypt; I rescued *you* from the hand of the Egyptians; I delivered *you* from the hand of all your oppressors; I drove them out before *you* and gave *you* their land; I said to *you*, "I am the LORD your God."

And then this last bit: But *you* have not listened to me.

There is only one response to this prophetic encouragement: repentance.

Might we begin to understand the "you" as us? All of these words are true for us, not metaphorically or by way of analogy to Jesus and the cross (though it certainly be true) but historically. We need this bigger story. Can we bring this history into our right here, right now reality? Could we allow this text to address us today? And might we allow this call to repentance to pierce our hearts? It's interesting how God first wants to address us before addressing me. I have this growing conviction that God must first speak to us personally before he can speak to me individually. Grapple with the nuance of that pondering today. The story of the Bible is not the story of a loose federation of individuals doing great things for God throughout history but the story of a banded people caught up in the bonded triune God doing incredible things through them for his glory and their growth and others' good.

The Prayer

God our Father, we are getting the picture that you are more interested in we than in just me. We sense there is this way you want to locate us and work with us within a bigger context of others. We sense you will need to break our fierce and rugged individualism in order to bring us home into a people. That scares us. We like control. We are comfortable with me, myself, and I—with you, of course. Lead us to the place that is both corporate and personal. Lead us to the "we" where we will become a different kind of me. We pray in Jesus' name, who with you and the Holy Spirit reign as one God forever and ever, amen.

The Question

• Go back to that series of "you" statements and read them aloud so your ears can hear them actually spoken in direct address—not individually but personally, with the understanding that the "you" is a corporate you.

6 The Movement from Timidity to Temerity

JUDGES 6:11–12 | The angel of the LORD came and sat down under the oak in Ophrah that belonged to Joash the Abiezrite, where his son Gideon was threshing wheat in a winepress to keep it from the Midianites. When the angel of the LORD appeared to Gideon, he said, "The LORD is with you, mighty warrior."

Consider This

Previously, in the promised land, the people of God found themselves in severe oppression. They were hiding in caves and clefts in rocks. The newest war machine à la the latest military technology had been unleashed on them: camels. They had been turned into the modern-day equivalent of Sherman tanks. Israel was defenseless. The people were desperate. Their desperation brought them to God, and God sent them words of encouragement through a prophet.

Today an angel of the Lord steps onto the stage of human history. I love how the Bible tells the story as history rather than mythology. No "once upon a time" here.

The angel of the LORD came and sat down under the oak in Ophrah that belonged to Joash the Abiezrite . . .

We know that the angel "sat down" and where—under the oak in Ophrah—and not only that but who the oak belonged to—Joash the Abiezrite. So we have just been inserted into the scene where we can begin to see the details of desperation. Did you pick up on this?

. . . where his son Gideon was threshing wheat in a winepress to keep it from the Midianites.

Threshing wheat in a winepress. Wait! Don't we thresh wheat on a threshing floor? And don't we find threshing floors on hilltops where the wind can blow away the chaff when the grain is winnowed? Of course. It makes perfect sense now. A winepress is a small place where they put grapes so they could press them and get the grape juice out. Threshing wheat in a winepress! What a phrase. It is an idiom of fear and intimidation. This is what human nature does in response to being bullied by oppressors. This is how oppression works. It's not so much what's happening out there in the fields or the culture or wherever. It's the way we let the bullying into our hearts and slowly begin to accommodate the bully oppressor. You start threshing wheat in a winepress. You begin to take a different route home from school or sit in a different seat on the bus or make alliances with other bigger, meaner bullies, or whatever other self-preservation techniques you can use.

Until the angel of the Lord comes and sits down under the oak in Ophrah and begins to inject temerity into your timidity. (Okay, I had to look temerity up, too, but it's the right word.)

Our God is on a mission to encourage us, not so much because we need encouragement but because we have a massive mission in front of us. And he will encourage us in any way possible and by any means conceivable. He prefers to use human beings, but, if necessary, he will use angels.

It's interesting how the book of Hebrews begins with a discussion of angels and how Jesus is superior to the angels. He has made us a little lower than the angels and yet crowned us with glory and honor. Read Hebrews 1 and 2. He has hidden us in his Son, Jesus Christ, and filled us with his Spirit. Because of this, we are in a sense greater than the angels. We are his army of encouragement. We all desperately need to receive encouragement and give encouragement—every single day.

The Prayer

Father, thank you for the way the hard seasons press us into more desperation for you. Thank you for the way you intersect our lives through angels, especially when they come in the form of our friends and even strangers. Help us become such people in the lives of others—sitting down under the oak tree with them and sharing the courage of your kingdom. In Jesus' name, amen.

The Questions

- Where do you find yourself on the spectrum between timidity and temerity? How might you find yourself threshing wheat in a winepress these days?

Why It Will Take Courage to Become an Encourager

7

JUDGES 6:11–12 | The angel of the Lord came and sat down under the oak in Ophrah that belonged to Joash the Abiezrite, where his son Gideon was threshing wheat in a winepress to keep it from the Midianites. When the angel of the Lord appeared to Gideon, he said, "The Lord is with you, mighty warrior."

Consider This

So we are sitting under the oak in Ophrah that belongs to Joash the Abiezrite, and we are watching his son, Gideon, cramming scraps of what sheaves of wheat could be found in the trampled fields into a winepress and trying to separate the grain from the chaff without anyone noticing. It is a painful, pitiful sight to behold.

The angel of the Lord approaches Gideon. Into this timid, fearful shell of a man, the angel speaks these words: "The LORD is with you, mighty warrior."

It reminds me of one of my favorite Latin phrases from law school: *non sequitur*. It means a conclusion or statement that does not logically follow from the previous argument or statement. Gideon threshing wheat in a winepress; the Lord is with you, mighty warrior.

Gideon sheepishly looks over his shoulder to see whom the angel might be talking to. When he discovers no one else is there, he responds with this: "'Pardon me, my lord,' Gideon replied, 'but if the LORD is with us, why has all this happened to us? Where are all his wonders that our ancestors told us about when they said, 'Did not the LORD bring us up out of Egypt?'" (Judg. 6:13).

Gideon believed in God. We see it clearly in his words. He heard the prophet's earlier proclamation of God's mighty deeds in the past. Rather than receiving the prophet's rebuke—"I said to you, 'I am the LORD your God; do not worship the gods of the Amorites, in whose land you live.' But you have not listened to me" (Judg. 6:10)—Gideon had hardened his heart. Look at his response: "But now the LORD has abandoned us and given us into the hand of Midian" (v. 13).

Gideon still believed in God, but he no longer believed God. Like so many of us, he had heard the stories about God, but he had not heard from God. This is where encouragement comes into play.

"The Lord is with you, mighty warrior."

This is pure encouragement. The angel does not see what the world sees, which is a version of what Gideon sees himself to be. The angel sees what God sees. The angel has come to personally present God's point of view on Gideon.

Now, I want to track out our earlier definition of biblical encouragement.

> To encourage in the biblical sense of the term is to stand in the stead and agency of Jesus, participating in the work of the Holy Spirit, to minister grace to human beings at the level of their inner person, communicating, conveying, and imparting life, love, courage, comfort, consolation, joy, peace, hope, faith, and other dispensations and manifestations of the kingdom of heaven as the moment invites or requires.

An encourager must learn to see others as God sees them and to persist in making that vision personally and particularly known. This means the encourager must learn not merely to speak about God with people but to speak for God into people. It means the miracle of encouragement must first happen in and for us. It will take courage to become an encourager. That's what's going on here with Gideon.

The Prayer

Father, it first humbles us and then scares us that you might want to speak through us to others—that you yourself would encourage someone else through us. We know we must first open ourselves to be encouraged by others in this same way. We are used to speaking a good word about you, but speaking for you strikes us as another thing entirely. We will need courage even to become an encourager. Come, Holy Spirit, and prepare us. In Jesus' name, amen.

The Questions

- Can you put yourself into Gideon's shoes in this encounter? What does that feel like to you?

8 From the Back Row of the Balcony to the Front at the Altar

JUDGES 6:15 | "Pardon me, my lord," Gideon replied, "but how can I save Israel? My clan is the weakest in Manasseh, and I am the least in my family."

Consider This

In my first year of law school, I faced the real prospect of academic failure for the first time in my life. One's entire grade in a class rests on the three-hour final exam alone, and the grading was done in an anonymous manner as one signs their exam with a preassigned secret number rather than their name. In those weeks leading up to the end of the first semester, my Sunday church attendance picked up quite a bit.

I am destined to remember one of those Sundays for the rest of my life and into eternity. I was in my usual seat on the back pew of the balcony. When I realized there was a guest preacher that day, I began to make my way to the door. I loved the senior pastor, who at that time was Dr. Jack Wilson, and his "good news that makes a difference!" Somehow, the gravity of the Holy Spirit held me in place.

The preacher turned out to be Rev. Wesley Putnam, and he entered the sanctuary dressed in full Bible character mode. He enacted the role of—you guessed it—Gideon. Everything I know about Gideon I learned that morning. I shall never forget it. For somehow in the miraculous mystery of the Word of God becoming enfleshed in this traveling evangelist, I not only met Gideon, but I also met God in a new way. And I not only met God in a deep way, but I also met myself in a new way. It was on that day, on the back row at the top of the balcony, I heard God saying to me, "The Lord is with you, mighty warrior."

And I knew he was calling my life into his purposes for the world. The thin clichéd veneer of "God's wonderful plan for my life" became a compelling and consuming invitation to lay down my life for God's purposes in the earth. And it was a long walk from the top row of the balcony to the altar at the front of that church.

In fact, I am still walking. And something tells me you are too.

I want to say something that will come as a big relief to many of you and perhaps as a shock. You have not missed

God's wonderful plan for your life. How do I know? Because God doesn't have a wonderful plan for your life. It is not some super-specific job or vocation or career path, and if you miss that, you've missed the plan. God has a plan all right—but it is not for your life. It's just the opposite. Your life is for his plan.

The LORD is with you, mighty warrior!

This is not a semantical turn of phrase. It is a flipping of the script. God has given you a life, right where you are, for his plan and purposes. And his plan and purposes are for your life to become so completely and utterly and over-whelmingly filled with his life and light and love that you become the most incredibly generous and encouraging and uncontainable blessing of a human being that people around you have ever seen. God's plan is to make you so filled with grace and truth and goodness and kindness that your children hardly recognize you anymore, that your parents have to do a double take.

The LORD is with you, mighty warrior!

The point is not to stress out over some specific plan you have to get right. The goal is to 100 percent give your life back to God, to give up your rights to yourself, to let go of your self-oriented ambitions, to walk away from the tower of Babel that your life has become, leaving it on the plains of Shinar, and abandon yourself to God. Does this mean a career change? It may, but probably not. God is far less interested in disrupting your plans than he is interested in erupting his life into your life. This is not about doing great things for God. It is about Jesus doing great things in you. It is high time we began seeing the will of God as a life of adventures and special assignments rather than as job descriptions and career paths.

Gideon was a farmer who was given an assignment that took him on an adventure. He knew he didn't have what it would take. He was about to learn that God did. He had to once again make the turn from believing in God to believing God. He needed courage. He simply needed to be encouraged. That's what you and I need. It takes encouragement to get from the back of the balcony to the front at the altar.

The Lord is with you, mighty warrior!

The Prayer

Father, thank you for Gideon, unimpressive, under-confident, unqualified, and underwhelming. Thank you for picking Gideon, because it increases our confidence that you might pick someone like us. Thank you for picking people like Gideon through whom you can demonstrate your goodness and display your glory. We want our lives to be for your plan. We want to flip the script. We want this life like Jesus—that is too good to be true and yet is true not because of us but because of you. Come, Holy Spirit, and lead us on. In Jesus' name, amen.

The Question

- What do you think of this flipped phrase—from "God's plan for my life" to "my life for God's plan"?

9 Unlearning Strengths; Embracing Weaknesses

JUDGES 6:15 | "Pardon me, my lord," Gideon replied, "but how can I save Israel? My clan is the weakest in Manasseh, and I am the least in my family."

Consider This

Why is it that our response to a word like "The Lord is with you, mighty warrior" tends to be "'Pardon me, my lord . . . but how can I save Israel? My clan is the weakest in Manasseh, and I am the least in my family'"?

It is strangely reminiscent of that time God called Moses. "Moses said to the Lord, 'Pardon your servant, Lord. I have never been eloquent, neither in the past nor since you have spoken to your servant. I am slow of speech and tongue'" (Ex. 4:10). And later this: "But Moses said, 'Pardon your servant, Lord. Please send someone else'" (Ex. 4:13).

I mean, do we really think the God of heaven and earth involves us because of our qualifications and strengths and superpowers? What if he involves us because of his qualifications and strengths and superpowers? What if he looks for the kind of people through whom to work such that it is clear who is who and who is doing what? It reminds me of what Paul said: "But we have this treasure in jars of clay to show that this all-surpassing power is from God and not from us" (2 Cor. 4:7). On another occasion he put it this way: "My message and my preaching were not with wise and persuasive words, but with a demonstration of the Spirit's power, so that your faith might not rest on human wisdom, but on God's power" (1 Cor. 2:4–5).

Paul had enormous qualifications and strengths and superpowers, but he had to unlearn them. What if our worldly qualifications are actually disqualifications in the kingdom of God? What if it's actually our weaknesses that most qualify us to walk and work with God? Paul was super educated, super competent, and super skilled, and yet he would come to say this: "Therefore I will boast all the more gladly about my weaknesses, so that Christ's power may rest on me. That is why, for Christ's sake, I delight in weaknesses, in insults, in hardships, in persecutions, in difficulties. For when I am weak, then I am strong" (2 Cor. 12:9b–10).

Something about God seems to love and even be drawn to human weakness. Yet we live in a world with a value system that is magnetically drawn to human strength. In fact, if we are honest, we are much more drawn to strengths in people than weaknesses. If we perceive ourselves to have a lack of strength or qualification to do something, we tend to shy away from it. "Find someone else," we say. Why? Could it be because we fear failure? And why do we fear failure? Could it be that we have our sense of identity and worth bound up with our performance and success and reputation? What if our deepest worth to God is actually not connected to our strengths but to our weaknesses?

I think one of the hardest things most of us have to learn is to embrace our weaknesses. Even harder sometimes is embracing the weaknesses of others. It's why encouragement is so important. What if we learned to encourage one another more in our weaknesses—to embrace them—than in our strengths and building them?

This seems pretty upside down, doesn't it? But then so does Jesus, right?

"But he said to me, 'My grace is sufficient for you, for my power is made perfect in weakness'" (2 Cor. 12:9).

The Prayer

Father, we struggle to admit it, but the truth is that we are weak and poor and needy. Thank you for being okay with this central feature of humanity. Help us to be okay with it. Even better, teach us to glory in it. We want to learn to embrace our weaknesses so that we become the kind of people through whom you can demonstrate your strengths. Come, Holy Spirit, and bring us this transformation of mind and heart. In Jesus' name, amen.

The Questions

- How are you with this whole upside-down teaching about weakness? How are you with your own weaknesses? What about the weaknesses of others?

Change of Life Begins with Change of Heart

10

JUDGES 6:20–24 | The angel of God said to him, "Take the meat and the unleavened bread, place them on this rock, and pour out the broth." And Gideon did so. Then the angel of the LORD touched the meat and the unleavened bread with the tip of the staff that was in his hand. Fire flared from the rock, consuming the meat and the bread. And the angel of the LORD disappeared. When Gideon realized that it was the angel of the LORD, he exclaimed, "Alas, Sovereign LORD! I have seen the angel of the LORD face to face!"

But the LORD said to him, "Peace! Do not be afraid. You are not going to die."

So Gideon built an altar to the LORD there and called it The LORD Is Peace. To this day it stands in Ophrah of the Abiezrites.

Consider This

If we might draw a word of encouragement from the story of Gideon thus far, it would be this: God chooses the unlikely to accomplish the impossible.

If we were to draw a second word of encouragement from today's text, it would be this one: a change of life only begins with a change of heart.

It would seem that taking on one's oppressive enemies would begin with a battle plan against them, the building of an army, and the development of some new battle strategy. In

God's kingdom, deliverance from enemies does not begin on the battlefield but in the heart. It does not begin by changing what is outside but what is inside.

The first step for Gideon to lead the people to deliverance from the Midianites was not an act of war but an act of worship. Gideon had to bring his own life from its own divided loyalties to the place of the undivided heart.

So Gideon built an altar to the LORD there and called it The LORD Is Peace. To this day it stands in Ophrah of the Abiezrites.

Gideon made peace with God. Gideon made the shift from believing in God to believing God. It would take some more reassurances, but here is where he crossed over.

So may I ask you the question? Have you crossed over? Have you moved from the passive place of believing in God and into the active faith of believing God?

The Prayer

Father, we know our hearts are divided. We want to be wholeheartedly and undividedly yours. Jesus, we belong to you. So we pray in the Spirit with the psalmist for you to search us and know our hearts. Test us and know our anxious thoughts. See if there is any offensive way in us, and lead us in the way everlasting. In Jesus' name, amen.

The Questions

- What divides your heart? Do you aspire to wholeheartedness? Are you willing to cast aside any and all other allegiances but to God alone?

Revolution Begins with Reform at the Home Office

11

JUDGES 6:25–26 | That same night the Lord said to him, "Take the second bull from your father's herd, the one seven years old. Tear down your father's altar to Baal and cut down the Asherah pole beside it. Then build a proper kind of altar to the Lord your God on the top of this height. Using the wood of the Asherah pole that you cut down, offer the second bull as a burnt offering."

Consider This

Reviewing our words of encouragement from the story of Gideon so far:

1. God chooses the unlikely to accomplish the impossible.

2. A change of life only begins with a change of heart.

Today we come to yet a third encouraging word—or at least it is a word that requires encouragement to undertake. Yet before that, let's once again revisit our working definition of biblical encouragement:

> To encourage in the biblical sense of the term is to stand in the stead and agency of Jesus, participating in the work of the Holy Spirit, to minister grace to human beings at the level of their inner person, communicating, conveying, and imparting life, love, courage, comfort, consolation, joy, peace, hope, faith, and other

dispensations and manifestations of the kingdom of
heaven as the moment invites or requires.

Now to the challenging encouragement from today's text:

3. Revolution begins with reform at the home office.

Tear down your father's altar to Baal . . .

Whatever Gideon was hoping he might hear from God, I
can assure you it was not this. It reminds me of that time as a
kid when my best friend took it upon himself to throw away
an entire carton of his father's cigarettes.

*Tear down your father's altar to Baal and cut down the
Asherah pole beside it.*

Here's how I imagine Gideon's initial response went: "Come
on, Lord. We made peace. Remember our altar moments? You
and me are back now. Things are good. Cozy even. Can we
just work on having some better devotional times together?
Why do you have to take it here so all of a sudden? This is not
what I signed on for."

And that's the problem, isn't it? We want God to comfort us
in our problematic life. We want him to bring the cozy into
our chaos, to hold our hand, to make it better. In this frame,
faith becomes more escape than engagement. We must
remember verse 4 and what drove us to our knees to begin
with: "They [the Midianites, Amalekites, and other eastern
peoples] camped on the land and ruined the crops all the
way to Gaza and did not spare a living thing for Israel, neither
sheep nor cattle nor donkeys."

Even worse is verse 2, which reminds us how we allowed
ourselves to deal with such oppression: "Because the power

of Midian was so oppressive, the Israelites prepared shelters for themselves in mountain clefts, caves and strongholds."

There is only one reason the people of God find themselves exiled in their own home. It's because their home has become compromised through allegiances and alliances with other gods, false teaching, counterfeit gospels, and idolatrous ideologies. The problem is not out there in the culture. That's the symptom. The problem is in here. After all, it is the very first commandment: "You shall have no other gods before me" (Ex. 20:3).

Revolution begins with reform in the home office.

Tear down your father's altar to Baal and cut down the Asherah pole beside it.

This takes enormous courage. There is perhaps no more essential encouragement that we need to receive and to give to others than this.

Revolution begins with reform in the home office: "For it is time for judgment to begin with God's household" (1 Peter 4:17a).

The Prayer

Father, let the revolution of awakening begin with reform in our hearts and at our home offices. Where have we compromised our allegiance to your sovereignty by some alliance with a lesser god, some other solution that promises comfort or prosperity? Is it money or some other addiction that has trapped us and made me us exiles in our own homes? So we continue to pray, Lord Jesus, send your Spirit to search us and know our hearts. Test us and know our anxious thoughts. See if there is any offensive way in us, and lead us in the way everlasting. In Jesus' name, amen.

The Question

- Where are your altars to Baal? Remember, they are easier to spot in your neighbor's house. Never start there. Always begin with your heart and your home. "Then you will see clearly . . ."

12 The Story of Two Altars

JUDGES 6:27–29 | So Gideon took ten of his servants and did as the LORD told him. But because he was afraid of his family and the townspeople, he did it at night rather than in the daytime.

In the morning when the people of the town got up, there was Baal's altar, demolished, with the Asherah pole beside it cut down and the second bull sacrificed on the newly built altar!

They asked each other, "Who did this?"

Consider This

This was *very* bold. Gideon took his dad's staff to destroy his dad's shrine. Who can fault him for doing this under the cover of night?

This is a story of two altars. Let's remember from yesterday: "Take the second bull from your father's herd, the one seven years old. Tear down your father's altar to Baal and cut down the Asherah pole beside it. Then build a proper kind of altar to the LORD your God on the top of this height. Using the wood of the Asherah pole that you cut down, offer the second bull as a burnt offering" (vv. 25–26).

Remember how many years Israel had suffered under Midianite oppression? Hint #1: it's in verse 1. Hint #2: it's as many years as the bull we shall call "Deuce" had been alive. Coincidence? Not on your life.

So Gideon tore down the altar to Baal, the god who was no god at all, and cut down the Asherah pole to the goddess. These were so-called fertility gods who promised flourishing life for all who would make sacrifices to serve them. Whatever it is in the world we turn to for life, safety, security, prosperity, and the flourishing good life, whatever alliances we are willing to forge or allegiances we will deign to pledge or oaths we will stoop to swear—those become our altars to Baal and Asherah. And something in us is willing to let this comparison live in the undefined place of a loose metaphor for a very long time. The din of idolatrous worship will eventually drown out everything save the desperation of the worshipper. And here's the good news: though it be seven years or seventy, it is never too late to tear down the altar to Baal and build a proper altar to God.

Now, here's the critical piece today. Notice where the "proper kind of altar to the LORD your God" gets built: "Then build a proper kind of altar to the LORD your God on the top of this height. Using the wood of the Asherah pole that you cut down, offer the second bull as a burnt offering" (v. 26).

The great seduction is to build the altar to the living God alongside the altar to a dead god (a.k.a. an idol). No one much minds Jesus as long as there is an "and" put before his name. With Jesus, it is always an "or." To say Jesus is Lord is to say Jesus or everything else. But then he is so good to come back around and tell us that if we will seek first his kingdom and his righteousness, he will provide everything else we could possibly need. It's why Jesus says it is very difficult for a wealthy person to inherit the kingdom of God—not because they have wealth but because their wealth has them. And who among us does not idolize wealth?

It's easy to build an altar to God alongside the other shrines in our lives. It takes enormous courage to tear down our altars to the lesser gods and to build a proper altar to the Lord your God. What a sign it is, though, when the stuff of the old altars becomes the fuel for the flames for the new altar. Oh my. These become the fires of great awakening, one by one, heart by heart, home by home, church by church, city by city.

There is a mighty roar of repentance coming on the horizon. It is the realignment that leads to unspeakable joy. Who is ready? Who will go first?

The Prayer

Father, we believe this is true, and yet we are still not quite willing to see it in ourselves. Where are the altars to the false gods and idols in our hearts? Search us, Holy Spirit. We pledge our repentance in advance. Where is our misplaced trust? Where are our misspent affections? Where are our lost longings? What is it apart from you that we think will make our lives work and even flourish? Jesus, we do not want to waste another day of our lives serving gods who are no gods at all, who promise life only to steal it. Grant us wisdom. Grant us courage for the facing of this hour. In Jesus' name, amen.

The Questions

- What gives you security in this life? Is it your wealth or the promise from pursuing it? Is it your appearance? Is it your network of relationships? Is it your name or your family heritage? Has it become the darkness of an addiction or a broken longing or an unholy attachment?

Aspiring to Tolerance and Inclusivity or Full of Grace and Truth?

13

JUDGES 6:29–32 | They asked each other, "Who did this?"

When they carefully investigated, they were told, "Gideon son of Joash did it."

The people of the town demanded of Joash, "Bring out your son. He must die, because he has broken down Baal's altar and cut down the Asherah pole beside it."

But Joash replied to the hostile crowd around him, "Are you going to plead Baal's cause? Are you trying to save him?

Whoever fights for him shall be put to death by morning! If Baal really is a god, he can defend himself when someone breaks down his altar." So because Gideon broke down Baal's altar, they gave him the name Jerub-Baal that day, saying, "Let Baal contend with him."

Consider This

They asked each other, "Who did this?"

"Bring out your son. He must die."

Could it be the ancient precursor to cancel culture?

That's what a culture built on an ideology of inclusivity invariably and ironically creates. Everyone is included. Every god, ideology, practice, group, teaching—except the one that holds any semblance of an exclusive claim. And the one who begins to order their life according to the requirements and commandments of a God who makes exclusive claims is headed for rough seas.

One would think Gideon would have been in the most trouble with his father, but it doesn't seem so from the text. Joash didn't believe in Baal. Something tells me his main-tenance of the altar to Baal was an accommodation to the surrounding culture, bowing to the spirit of the age if you will. Look what he says:

"If Baal really is a god, he can defend himself when someone breaks down his altar."

Not exactly an affirmation of faith, right? Joash neither believed Baal nor believed in him. He accommodated the spirit of the age. He did the acceptable thing in the eyes of the culture. The minute an exclusive God comes onto the scene of an inclusive pantheon, everything blows up. The culture and ideology of inclusivity can tolerate anything and everything under the sun except an exclusive God.

And isn't it amazing how much oppression a culture will tolerate and even propagate as long as every god, every ideology, every practice, every so-called truth gets a seat at the table?

Let's remember, though, awakening does not begin with attacks on the surrounding culture. It begins with reform at the home office. Though there was a public interest here, this was Joash's altar after all. And reform at the home office begins with our coming to grips with the one true God's exclusive claims to ownership of our hearts and our homes.

The God of the Bible demands an exclusive relationship with his people. He will not tolerate other gods, idols, and false ideologies. Why? Because he loves us with a love that will not allow us to be diminished. A divided heart leads to a divided life, which is unstable, unfruitful, and ultimately unsustainable. A divided heart is a confused heart, and a confused heart becomes a darkened heart, and a darkened heart becomes a dead heart. Competing loyalties inexorably become confused loyalties and lead to chaotic lives.

Here's the most interesting part: though a culture built on the ideology of inclusivity can tolerate everything except an exclusive God, an exclusive God and his people can not only tolerate the people of a hostile culture but embrace them. We can embrace those who disagree with us and resist us and even oppose us because we know who we are and whose we are. Because Jesus Christ is Lord, we don't cancel our enemies. We embrace them.

Here's the encouragement: we would be well-served to stop bashing the surrounding culture. We need to let judgment begin with our hearts and homes and houses of worship. In the end those who stand on the claim "Jesus is Lord" do not strive to be tolerant and inclusive. We aspire to become gracious and truthful. They are very different realities.

The Prayer

Father, help us understand what is being said here and what is not being said. Help us respond rather than react. Give us grace to begin with our homes. Come, Holy Spirit, and pierce the veil of the spirit of the age in which we live. We need clarity of vision and keenness of insight. We do not want to accommodate things that are not true in the interest of affirming everyone's truth. We do not want to accommodate false gods and falsehoods in the spirit of being tolerant and inclusive. We want to be like Jesus, full of grace and truth and abounding in steadfast love. In Jesus' name, amen.

The Questions

- Do you believe Jesus Christ is Lord? If so, why are you accommodating other gods? Will you examine your heart?

How to Know If You Are Doing Something Right

14

JUDGES 6:33–35 | Now all the Midianites, Amalekites and other eastern peoples joined forces and crossed over the Jordan and camped in the Valley of Jezreel. Then the Spirit of the LORD came on Gideon, and he blew a trumpet, summoning the Abiezrites to follow him. He sent messengers throughout Manasseh, calling them to arms, and also into Asher, Zebulun and Naphtali, so that they too went up to meet them.

Consider This

I never imagined I would go this long on this one story, but it is so irresistibly compelling I can't stop. We must see it through now. Honestly, the bit at the beginning with Gideon threshing wheat in a winepress and the angel addressing him as "mighty warrior" was the part that I wanted to expose given the larger "encourage one another" theme of the present series. The further I go in, however, something tells me that the Holy Spirit is himself encouraging people in strong and particular ways the further we go. So finish we will.

Let's get some perspective. After seven years of withering fire and unrelenting oppression, Israel cried out to the God of their ancestors for help. God sent a prophet. Then God sent an angel to a most unlikely figure: Gideon. Gideon obeyed the Lord's commands, which immediately made him public

45

enemy number one. Life had gone from bad to worse for Gideon. In today's text, we will see how Gideon's obedience to God made life worse for the whole country.

Now all the Midianites, Amalekites and other eastern peoples joined forces and crossed over the Jordan and camped in the Valley of Jezreel.

Interestingly, the Jezreel Valley is also known as the Valley of Megiddo, from which will later be derived the name *Armageddon*, the battle to end all battles. This is really bad for the people, and especially bad for Gideon, as there were probably lots of causal links being drawn by armchair quarterbacks between Gideon's destruction of the altar of Baal and the rising tide of these allied armies coming against them.

This is how it so often goes when someone finally stands up and takes a swing at evil. Evil swings back—and much harder. Things seem to go from bad to worse to worst. It can leave us wondering, did we hear from God wrongly? In truth, the increase of opposition is often the sign of confirmation that you heard correctly. This is why it is so essential that we strongly and consistently encourage anyone who is even remotely thinking about following Jesus beyond the scope of reasonable, benign church activity and leading a charge into enemy territory.

Gideon now has a target on his back, and he is being assaulted from within by his own people and also from without by enemy forces. Here is how Paul would describe Gideon's newfound precarious situation: "hard pressed on every side, but not crushed; perplexed, but not in despair; persecuted, but not abandoned; struck down, but not destroyed" (2 Cor. 4:8–9).

These are the ironic and unwanted signs you are doing something right, that you are onto the scent of the will of God. When we seek to obey the voice of God, we can expect a fight. Anytime anyone awakens from sleep and rises up to follow Jesus beyond the cozy confines of domesticated religion, they must be encouraged, for the armies of hell will come against that person.

Let me issue a caution though. It is easy and common (and dangerous and abusive) for a leader to demonize and vilify anyone who resists their leadership along these same lines. How do we know the difference? We must know the difference between resistance and opposition. Resistance to a proposal or plan of attack is most often a good thing. It helps to test, clarify, sharpen, and strengthen a plan. The sign of a mature leader is their ability to welcome resistance from others and receive influence. Opposition is a different matter. Opponents don't usually want to test, clarify, sharpen, or strengthen. They want to advance their own course and often for their own ends. Resistance should be welcomed. Opposition must be confronted. Knowing the difference is the secret sauce of wise leadership.

The Prayer

Father, we do feel hard pressed on every side. Convince us today that we are not going to be crushed. We do feel perplexed. Keep us out of the pit of despair. We often feel persecuted. Remind us we are never abandoned. And when it seems we are struck down, we will declare, "We are not destroyed." Come, Holy Spirit, and put on us the full armor of God so that when the day of evil comes, we may be able to stand our ground, and after we have done everything, to stand (Eph. 6:13). Show us how to wear and bear the armor in the surprising way of Jesus. In his name we pray, amen.

The Questions
- Who comes to mind as a person you need to encourage given today's reading? How will you encourage them?

15 Thoughts on Fleecing God

JUDGES 6:36–40 | Gideon said to God, "If you will save Israel by my hand as you have promised—look, I will place a wool fleece on the threshing floor. If there is dew only on the fleece and all the ground is dry, then I will know that you will save Israel by my hand, as you said." And that is what happened. Gideon rose early the next day; he squeezed the fleece and wrung out the dew—a bowlful of water.

Then Gideon said to God, "Do not be angry with me. Let me make just one more request. Allow me one more test with the fleece, but this time make the fleece dry and let the ground be covered with dew." That night God did so. Only the fleece was dry; all the ground was covered with dew.

Consider This

Everyone wants to know if this is a prescriptive text or a descriptive text. In other words, does it instruct us on how to relate to God in our attempts to discern his will, or does it merely describe how Gideon related to God in this instance?

I believe the text is far more descriptive than prescriptive. Why? If there is one thing we need to remember about Gideon, it is where God found him: threshing wheat in a winepress and saying things like, "If the LORD is with us, why has all this happened to us? Where are all his wonders that our ancestors told us about when they said, 'Did not the LORD bring us up out of Egypt?' But now the LORD has abandoned us and given us into the hand of Midian" (Judg. 6:13).

Gideon was far from a paragon of faith. He was an average farmer trying to scratch out a living in a desperate situation. Gideon was the equivalent of a B-team benchwarmer on the junior high football team who was not only skipping high school and college but being drafted straight into the NFL. It was a bit beyond absurd. He wasn't ready for the assignment, and his responses tell the story. He wanted to be sure. He needed confirmation. He was desperate for a sign, and another sign, and another sign. And God was so good to give him what he needed. It was a combination of an extraordinary set of circumstances and a God who meets us and works with us as he finds us.

Honestly, though, from my reading of Scripture, I don't think "fleecing" (or putting out a fleece) is the preferred method for discerning the heart and mind of the God of heaven and earth. So what does God want from us?

In a word: maturity.

Our Father wants us to grow up into the deep likeness of his Son, Jesus, anchored in his Word, animated by his Spirit, abiding in his presence, attached to his friends, and activated in his kingdom.

I like how Paul puts it in Romans 12:1: "Therefore, I urge you, brothers and sisters, in view of God's mercy, to offer your bodies as a living sacrifice, holy and pleasing to God—this is your true and proper worship."

Then he teaches us how to discern the will of God: "Do not conform to the pattern of this world, but be transformed by the renewing of your mind. Then you will be able to test and approve what God's will is—his good, pleasing and perfect will" (Rom. 12:2).

Here's the encouragement: to know the will of God, don't put out a fleece. Surrender your life to Jesus and become the gloriously incredible person you were put on earth to be. Stop copying the world around you. Be consecrated to the God who would indwell you.

One more bit. It's good to see Gideon out of the winepress and back out on the threshing floor today, even with his fleece. He's not threshing wheat there yet, but he's making moves. This pleases God . . . every single time. What move will you make today? Let's encourage one another to stop asking God to show us signs of his readiness and start showing God signs of our readiness. That's what really thrills God's heart.

The Prayer

Father, we want maturity. We want to grow up into Christ. We know you aren't asking us to try harder but rather to simply give ourselves to you completely and wholeheartedly. We want to live our lives in you. We want to be built up in you. We want to be strengthened in you. We want to be who you saw when you created us. Thank you for meeting us where we are and working with what we have. Come, Holy Spirit, and awaken our spirits to the good, pleasing, and perfect will of God. In Jesus' name we pray, amen.

The Questions

- Where are you ready to stop conforming to the broken patterns of the world? How is the Holy Spirit leading you to "be transformed by the renewing of your mind"? What does a move look like today? How might you signal God with a sign of your readiness to go to the next place of obedience and faith?

16 The Battle for Our Whole Hearts

JUDGES 7:1–3 | Early in the morning, Jerub-Baal (that is, Gideon) and all his men camped at the spring of Harod. The camp of Midian was north of them in the valley near the hill of Moreh. The LORD said to Gideon, "You have too many men. I cannot deliver Midian into their hands, or Israel would boast against me, 'My own strength has saved me.' Now announce to the army, 'Anyone who trembles with fear may turn back and leave Mount Gilead.'" So twenty-two thousand men left, while ten thousand remained.

Consider This

Finally sufficiently confident in God's direction and favor, Gideon blew the trumpet, put out the call for freedom fighters, and look what happened: thirty-two thousand men reported for duty. Surely Gideon must have thought to himself, *Look what God did! Isn't God amazing!* Or maybe he thought, *Well, that's a good start against an army three times our size, but not nearly enough!* Pay very close attention to what God says here:

"You have too many men. I cannot deliver Midian into their hands, or Israel would boast against me, 'My own strength has saved me.'"

We want God and the big army. We want God and the fat endowment. We want God and the smartest, most talented people in the room. And here's the biggest seduction of them all: we want to tell ourselves that God gave us the army and the endowment and the smartest, most talented people in the room, effectively merging the two into one. Then we find ourselves in this place of fuzzy faith where we say things like, "Look what God did," while quietly congratulating ourselves for all our hard work that made it possible.

"You have too many men. I cannot deliver Midian into their hands, or Israel would boast against me, 'My own strength has saved me.'"

Imagine God saying to you after your massive multi-year capital campaign, "You have too much money. Give two-thirds of it back." And according to the story as it will unfold, we would only just be getting started.

This is why God chooses a kid with a slingshot and no armor to take on the giant Goliath. This is why God picks a teenage girl in a nowhere town to carry his Son to term. This is why he calls a super-talented leader like Paul and teaches him all his qualifications are as worthless to God as a pile of garbage. Get a load of this:

> But God chose the foolish things of the world to shame the wise; God chose the weak things of the world to shame the strong. God chose the lowly things of this world and the despised things—and the things that are not—to nullify the things that are, so that no one may boast before him. (1 Cor. 1:27–29)

This is why the cross is foolishness to those who are perishing, but to us who are being saved it is the power of God.

I think God would rather receive a dollar from a million poor people who couldn't afford even that than to get a million dollars from a super-wealthy person who would never even miss it. Why? Because God doesn't need our power or our money or our talent. He wants our hearts. That's the encouragement today. Give him your whole heart.

It's why God's first altar call of the morning was done in reverse:

"Now announce to the army, 'Anyone who trembles with fear may turn back and leave Mount Gilead.' So twenty-two thousand men left, while ten thousand remained."

God is looking for our hearts, our wholehearted, all-in hearts. That's where great awakenings begin—with the ones who tremble not in fear but in awe of him alone.

The Prayer

Father, we want you to have our hearts. Yet we realize we need you to give us more access to our own hearts that we might grant that access back to you. Open the eyes of our hearts, Lord, to behold you, to fathom you, to be able to imagine just how good you are and loving and powerful and merciful. Come, Holy Spirit, awaken our hearts to the pure unadulterated reality of you that our lives might become an unfolding extravagant response to all that you are. In Jesus' name, amen.

The Questions

- How are you trusting God in a real way these days, with no backup plan? Where in your life do you fail if God does not intervene?

This Is a Story about God

17

JUDGES 7:4–6 | But the Lord said to Gideon, "There are still too many men. Take them down to the water, and I will thin them out for you there. If I say, 'This one shall go with you,' he shall go; but if I say, 'This one shall not go with you,' he shall not go."

So Gideon took the men down to the water. There the Lord told him, "Separate those who lap the water with their tongues as a dog laps from those who kneel down to drink." Three hundred of them drank from cupped hands, lapping like dogs. All the rest got down on their knees to drink.

Consider This

Can you even imagine this?

But the Lord said to Gideon, "There are still too many men. Take them down to the water, and I will thin them out for you there."

The shoe is solidly on the other foot now, isn't it? We have gone from Gideon testing God to God testing Gideon.

So Gideon took the men down to the water. There the Lord told him, "Separate those who lap the water with their tongues as a dog laps from those who kneel down to drink."

I've heard preachers try to churchsplain this to mean that those soldiers who cupped the water into their hands were the real warriors because they did not drop to their knees but stayed in a battle-ready position. Then we get this.

Three hundred of them drank from cupped hands, lapping like dogs. All the rest got down on their knees to drink.

Can you imagine? Three hundred tongue lappers! Yep! That should do the trick.

Let's make sure we are doing the same math here. Gideon started with ten servants from his father's staff. He issued the call to arms and fielded a team of thirty-two thousand. He let everyone who trembled in fear go home, which reduced the army by twenty-two thousand, leaving ten thousand. Now we are down to three hundred.

This is not a story about Gideon. It is certainly not a story about battle strategy or leadership. It is not even a story about faith (though Gideon does get an honorable mention in the famed Hall of Faith; see Hebrews 11:32). This is a story about God.

In fact, that is what the whole story of the Bible is about: the one true God of heaven and earth, Father, Son, and Holy Spirit. Over and over and over we try to make the Bible about us. Our main questions tend to be about us: How does this apply to my life? What is this telling me to do? How is this relevant? Those are just not really the questions the Bible is asking or answering. The Bible aspires first, middle, and last to do one thing: reveal God. The Word of God and the Spirit of God are ever working to reveal the eternal God to mortal human beings—to lift our eyes to the hills with the clarion query, "From where does our help come?"

Our help comes from the Lord, the maker of heaven and earth.

This is a story about God.

There is simply no one like him.

The Prayer

Father, we stand amazed and in awe of you. You, God. You alone. You are amazing, astounding, and the more we see you, the more we want to see you. Thank you for your Word and your Spirit and the gift of revelation. Help us to fathom you more today than we did yesterday, and then again tomorrow. That will be enough. In Jesus' name, amen.

The Question

- Think about the last sermon you heard (or preached). How much of it was really revealing who God is and what God is like and how God works, and how much of it was really more about people and, at best, indirectly about God? As a preacher, I live under conviction a lot on this very point.

How the Gift of Assurance Works

18

JUDGES 7:8–15 | So Gideon sent the rest of the Israelites home but kept the three hundred, who took over the provisions and trumpets of the others.

Now the camp of Midian lay below him in the valley. During that night the LORD said to Gideon, "Get up, go down against the camp, because I am going to give it into your hands. If you are afraid to attack, go down to the camp with your servant Purah and listen to what they are saying. Afterward, you will be encouraged to attack the camp." So he and Purah his servant went down to the outposts of the camp. The Midianites, the Amalekites and all the other eastern peoples had settled in the valley, thick as locusts. Their camels could no more be counted than the sand on the seashore.

Gideon arrived just as a man was telling a friend his dream. "I had a dream," he was saying. "A round loaf of barley bread came tumbling into the Midianite camp. It struck the tent with such force that the tent overturned and collapsed."

His friend responded, "This can be nothing other than the sword of Gideon son of Joash, the Israelite. God has given the Midianites and the whole camp into his hands."

When Gideon heard the dream and its interpretation, he bowed down and worshiped. He returned to the camp of Israel and called out, "Get up! The Lord has given the Midianite camp into your hands."

Consider This

So Gideon sent the rest of the Israelites home but kept the three hundred, who took over the provisions and trumpets of the others.

This is a story about God.

The Midianites, the Amalekites and all the other eastern peoples had settled in the valley, thick as locusts. Their camels could no more be counted than the sand on the seashore.

Yes, this is a story about God.

I wonder what you are facing right now and just how overwhelming the odds against you may be. You are likely tempted to try to win the war in the way the world would tell you the war must be won—by trying harder, by digging deeper, by building security and strength and all the other things. Perhaps someone is telling you that all you need is more faith, that somehow you are not believing enough. Let me be emphatic about this next statement: all of that is wrong.

This is not about standing in our strengths but glorying in our weakness. This is not about the quantity or even the quality of our faith. This is about the nature of our God. Hear Jesus on this point: "Truly I tell you, if you have faith as small as a mustard seed, you can say to this mountain, 'Move from here to there,' and it will move. Nothing will be impossible for you" (Matt. 17:20).

It is not about the quantity of one's faith. It is about the nature of one's God. The issue is in whom our faith is placed. Jesus chooses a seed so small it could hardly be seen in order to say, in essence, this is a story about God.

And look how good God is.

"If you are afraid to attack, go down to the camp with your servant Purah and listen to what they are saying. Afterward, you will be encouraged to attack the camp."

Notice the transformation afoot in Gideon. Gideon is not asking for more signs. Instead, God is encouraging Gideon with assurances. This is how it is supposed to work. God calls us to faith. Faith does not ask for a sign but simply obeys God. In response to obedience, God gives assurance to faith. This raises faith even higher. Now look what happens when Gideon acts on God's assurance.

Gideon arrived just as a man was telling a friend his dream. "I had a dream," he was saying. "A round loaf of barley bread came tumbling into the Midianite camp. It struck the tent with such force that the tent overturned and collapsed."

His friend responded, "This can be nothing other than the sword of Gideon son of Joash, the Israelite. God has given the Midianites and the whole camp into his hands."

When Gideon heard the dream and its interpretation, he bowed down and worshiped.

How awesome is that! Pay attention here. Gideon is worshipping God not based on the success of the mission but on the gift of God's assurance. It is as though God's encouragement to Gideon through this gift of assurance is as good as the victory itself. This is real faith, people. This is the faith that pleases God. "And without faith it is impossible to please God, because anyone who comes to him must believe that he exists and that he rewards those who earnestly seek him" (Heb. 11:6).

If you are out on a limb for Jesus, and I know many of you are, be encouraged—your faith pleases God very much. Take delight in his delight in you. Bow down and worship him now.

The Prayer

Come, let us worship and bow down. Let us kneel before the Lord our God, our Maker. For he is our God, and we are the people of his pasture and the sheep of his hand (Ps. 95:6–7).

Thank you, Jesus, for this great mystery of faith. The smallest seed of faith in the greatness of our God actually moves mountains. Thank you for not making it about our faith but about your greatness and glory. Come, Holy Spirit, and show us how to live in this place of faith all the time. In Jesus' name, amen.

The Questions

- Where are you needing assurance in your faith? Are you seeing the difference between asking for a sign before you have faith and receiving assurance after the obedience of faith? How would you articulate that? Can you tell a story of it?

Has Anybody Got a Trumpet?

19

JUDGES 7:16–21 | Dividing the three hundred men into three companies, he placed trumpets and empty jars in the hands of all of them, with torches inside.

"Watch me," he told them. "Follow my lead. When I get to the edge of the camp, do exactly as I do. When I and all who are with me blow our trumpets, then from all around the camp blow yours and shout, 'For the LORD and for Gideon.'"

Gideon and the hundred men with him reached the edge of the camp at the beginning of the middle watch, just after they had changed the guard. They blew their trumpets and broke the jars that were in their hands. The three companies blew the trumpets and smashed the jars. Grasping the torches in their left hands and holding in their right hands the trumpets they were to blow, they shouted, "A sword for the Lord and for Gideon!" While each man held his position around the camp, all the Midianites ran, crying out as they fled.

Consider This

Has anybody out there got a trumpet?

Three hundred men. Three hundred clay jars. Three hundred torches. And three hundred trumpets . . . against an army whose camels couldn't even be counted, not to mention their army.

And with this, our God defeated the armies of mighty Midian.

Trumpets figure prominently in the story of God.

Something about the trumpet sounds the very note of encouragement to the hearts of God's people.

> The Lord said to Moses, "Say to the Israelites: 'On the first day of the seventh month you are to have a day of sabbath rest, a sacred assembly commemorated with trumpet blasts. Do no regular work, but present a food offering to the Lord.'" (Lev. 23:23–25)

> Then have the trumpet sounded everywhere on the tenth day of the seventh month; on the Day of Atonement sound the trumpet throughout your land. (Lev. 25:9)

When you go into battle in your own land against an enemy who is oppressing you, sound a blast on the trumpets. Then you will be remembered by the Lord your God and rescued from your enemies. (Num. 10:9)

The seven priests carrying the seven trumpets went forward, marching before the ark of the Lord and blowing the trumpets. The armed men went ahead of them and the rear guard followed the ark of the Lord, while the trumpets kept sounding. (Josh. 6:13)

When the trumpets sounded, the army shouted, and at the sound of the trumpet, when the men gave a loud shout, the wall collapsed; so everyone charged straight in, and they took the city. (Josh. 6:20)

Blow the trumpet in Zion;
  sound the alarm on my holy hill.

Let all who live in the land tremble,
  for the day of the Lord is coming.
It is close at hand— (Joel 2:1)

The seventh angel sounded his trumpet, and there were loud voices in heaven, which said:

"The kingdom of the world has become
  the kingdom of our Lord and of his Messiah,
  and he will reign for ever and ever." (Rev. 11:15)

Listen, I tell you a mystery: We will not all sleep, but we will all be changed—in a flash, in the twinkling of an eye, at the last trumpet. For the trumpet will sound, the dead will be raised imperishable, and we will be changed. (1 Cor. 15:51–52)

The first trumpet we see in Scripture, however, is a great mystery: "On the morning of the third day there was thunder and lightning, with a thick cloud over the mountain, and a very loud trumpet blast. Everyone in the camp trembled." (Ex. 19:16)

Best we can tell, this was the very trumpet of God—sounded by God himself! "As the sound of the trumpet grew louder and louder, Moses spoke and the voice of God answered him." (Ex. 19:19)

And something tells me the final trumpet, "the last trumpet," will also be sounded by God himself: "Listen, I tell you a mystery: We will not all sleep, but we will all be changed—in a flash, in the twinkling of an eye, at the last trumpet. For the trumpet will sound, the dead will be raised imperishable, and we will be changed." (1 Cor. 15:51–52)

The first and only real instrument I ever learned to play was the trumpet.

I'm thinking of getting it back out.

Anybody out there got a trumpet and want to join me?

The Prayer

Father, thank you for the blast of the trumpet. Would you bring it back? Could the sounds of the trumpet be heard again among the people of God? Let it become the instrument of awakening. Let it become the very note of encouragement. Come, Holy Spirit, and sound the trumpet of God in our day. In Jesus' name, amen.

The Question

- How has this story of God (a.k.a. the story of Gideon) encouraged you?

The Seductive Hell of a Predictable Situation

20

NUMBERS 13:1–3A, 17–20 | The LORD said to Moses, "Send some men to explore the land of Canaan, which I am giving to the Israelites. From each ancestral tribe send one of its leaders."

So at the LORD's command Moses sent them out from the Desert of Paran. . . .

When Moses sent them to explore Canaan, he said, "Go up through the Negev and on into the hill country. See what the land is like and whether the people who live there are strong or weak, few or many. What kind of land do they live in? Is it good or bad? What kind of towns do they live in? Are they unwalled or fortified? How is the soil? Is it fertile or poor? Are there trees in it or not? Do your best to bring back some of the fruit of the land." (It was the season for the first ripe grapes.)

Consider This

Today we come to another text from which we can glean lessons on what it means to "encourage one another daily, as long as it is called 'Today'" (Heb. 3:13).

We come to the famed story of the twelve spies. I call it "The Minority Report." Encouragement in the biblical sense of the term most often comes in the form of a minority report. The will, calling, and assignments of God are most often unconventional and occasionally downright outlandish. The math rarely adds up. It requires a suspension of rational judgment and an immersion into the imagination of Jesus and the kingdom of heaven. God fights swords with trumpets. Then he takes the swords and beats them into plowshares.

Setting the stage: The Israelites had journeyed out of Egypt, miraculously walked through the Red Sea on dry ground, been led by a pillar of cloud by day and a pillar of fire by night, fed manna every morning and quail in the evening, drank water from rocks, and the list goes on. As they neared the promised land, God led Moses to develop a reconnaissance mission with twelve spies to scout out the territory.

The wilderness had not been easy. It never is. This story will show us something deeply embedded in the human condition—how people will readily choose a known misery over an unknown possibility. There is something deep and dark about the law of sin and death that will lead even redeemed people to return to darkness and death, even slavery and abuse, rather than risk freedom, flourishing, and joy by choosing an unknown possibility and an uncertain future. This is why encouragement is so critical to both give and receive. My mentor Maxie Dunnam puts it best: "Most people prefer the hell of a predictable situation rather than risk the joy of an unpredictable one."

Many people we meet, every single day, are fighting a difficult battle, confronting hard circumstances, facing an uncertain future. It is why we must encourage one another daily, as long as it is called "today," so that we will not be hardened by the deceitfulness of sin.

The Prayer

Father, we get it. There is something about a predictable future, even if it is a hellish one, that can give us comfort. We get used to it. We lose sight of what once was or what could be. It is so darkly seductive to slowly acclimate to the ever-dimming light. And the longer we live in this place, the harder it becomes to even imagine what you can do. Come, Holy Spirit, and bring awakening. Teach us to encourage each other in ways that awaken us to your possibilities and stand on your promises. Turn our eyes upon Jesus. In his name we pray, amen.

The Questions

- Are you living in a predictably less than promising and hopeful situation right now? Know anyone who is? Are you open to deep encouragement in said situation? Are you ready to encourage others in truly empowered ways?

21 Exploring the Unpredictable Life of the Promises of God

NUMBERS 13:21–25 | So they went up and explored the land from the Desert of Zin as far as Rehob, toward Lebo Hamath. They went up through the Negev and came to Hebron, where Ahiman, Sheshai and Talmai, the descendants of Anak, lived. (Hebron had been built seven years before Zoan in Egypt.) When they reached the Valley of Eshkol, they cut off a branch bearing a single cluster of grapes. Two of them carried it on a pole between them, along with some pomegranates and figs. That place was called the Valley of Eshkol because of the cluster of grapes the Israelites cut off there. At the end of forty days they returned from exploring the land.

Consider This

It's today again, which means it is another opportunity to encourage one another.

I wonder how many of us find ourselves in a situation we didn't really choose, in a scenario that chose us. Something happened somewhere along the way to interrupt our best-laid plans. Maybe it was cancer or divorce or the unexpected and perhaps untimely death of a loved one. Maybe it was the loss of a job or a community in an unforeseen move. Maybe it was the slow-rising tide of an addiction; what began as a glass of wine in the evening has become boxes of wine every week.

Certainly, the global pandemic has pushed all of us into ways of wilderness life we would never have chosen. We have taken to watching church on TV as if church were something that could be watched, and we wonder if we will ever really go back. In short, we have been pushed into ways of life we could slowly and easily settle into, setting up house in a wilderness never meant to be our home.

This was the story for the people of God in the book of Numbers. They hated life in the wilderness, and yet it had become their life. They grumbled and complained about everything almost constantly, yet not only would they come to settle for life outside of the promises of God, but they would even make themselves at home there. No one ever consciously chooses to live beneath the promises of God, though. They just don't choose the faith it takes to claim and pursue the promised life.

That's what we will face here with God's people in the wilderness. And that's what we are facing in our own lives right now. Will we choose God and the promised life and the faith it requires of us, or will we quietly not choose at all and settle for the striving mediocrity and comfortable existence of a predictable life? The bad news: we only have one shot at this life, and it is passing us by. The good news: we get to choose, and the opportunities to choose keep coming around, until they don't. Here is my deep encouragement for your heart (and mine) right here and right now:

> This is why it is said:
> "Wake up, sleeper,
>   rise from the dead,
>   and Christ will shine on you." (Eph. 5:14)

Many of us need to take a reconnaissance mission into the promised land of possibilities in our own lives. It's time to shake off the grave clothes of the pandemic and all it has meant. We can't settle for this present wilderness and succumb to the deep tendency to make ourselves at home here. Nor can we go back to normal. We must press on toward the promise. It is time to explore the unpredictable life of the promises of God.

Now I want you to get a picture of the veritable farmers market these twelve explorers brought back with them from this land of promise.

When they reached the Valley of Eshkol, they cut off a branch bearing a single cluster of grapes. Two of them carried it on a pole between them, along with some pomegranates and figs.

The Prayer

Father, we are tired and weary of this season of life. We didn't see it coming, and we don't see a way out. We confess, we are slowly getting used to it. And we know if we don't wake up, we will gradually settle for it. Let all of this shaking we have been through accrue to awakening to you, Jesus. We are desperate for you, Lord. Come, Holy Spirit, and take us into the new land of the new creation life you made us for. In Jesus' name we pray, amen.

The Questions

- Do you find yourself slowly settling for a life beneath the promises of God? What are you turning to in order to prop your life up these days? Don't you want better? Will you risk simple honesty today? Name the place. Make an altar to Jesus. Name the altar. Get ready for deliverance.

On the Essential Practice of Preemptive Obedience

22

NUMBERS 13:26–29 | They came back to Moses and Aaron and the whole Israelite community at Kadesh in the Desert of Paran. There they reported to them and to the whole assembly and showed them the fruit of the land. They gave Moses this account: "We went into the land to which you sent us, and it does flow with milk and honey! Here is its fruit. But the people who live there are powerful, and the cities are fortified and very large. We even saw descendants of Anak there. The Amalekites live in the Negev; the Hittites, Jebusites and Amorites live in the hill country; and the Canaanites live near the sea and along the Jordan."

Consider This

Let's remember our big banner text flying over this entire series: "But encourage one another daily, as long as it is called 'Today,' so that none of you may be hardened by sin's deceitfulness" (Heb. 3:13).

Reverse translation: If we do not encourage one another daily, as long as it is called "today," we may be hardened by sin's deceitfulness.

The exploratory spy mission lasted for forty days, and then the spies returned to the wilderness camp. Imagine how eager everyone must have been to hear the report. They could not have imagined how consequential this report and their response would be.

They gave Moses this account: "We went into the land to which you sent us, and it does flow with milk and honey! Here is its fruit."

So far, so good. Then we come to conjunction junction. And we get the dreaded "but."

1. But the people who live there are powerful;

2. The cities are fortified;

3. The cities are very large;

4. We even saw descendants of Anak there;

5. The Amalekites live in the Negev;

6. The Hittites, Jebusites, and Amorites live in the hill country; and

7. The Canaanites live near the sea and along the Jordan.

Can you feel the oxygen slowly being sucked out of the room?

We have slipped from simple reporting to an analysis of pros and cons. We do it all the time. We go from "God will be faithful to fulfill his promise" to the Benjamin Franklin method with a "reasons why" column and a "reasons why not" column.

When God says go, it is appropriate to "count the cost," but there is a vast difference in counting the cost and doing cost-benefit analysis. I want to be very clear about something at this point: when God gives a direction or an assignment, we don't determine its legitimacy or veracity by running spreadsheets to see if it makes sense. God's will and assignments rarely make sense in the world's way of making sense of things. We must determine to obey first, before we even get the assignment. Then it's not a question of if we will obey but how we will execute on our predetermined obedience.

There will be plenty of time to count the costs, and they must be counted. That said, we never count the cost to determine if we can afford it or if we have what it takes. Perhaps one of the biggest signs something *is* God's will is we know that we can't afford it and we are certain that we don't have what it takes. (Or do we need to call Gideon back to the witness stand?)

Most of the effort and energy to do the will of God I've seen and been a part of in my life has been done in God's name but in man's calculus. It's been governed more by accountants than apostles. It's been run more by best practices than bold prophets. Good work can happen that way for sure. I'm just not sure we should be calling it "God's work." I don't know about you, but I'm ready to be part of God's work.

The Prayer

Father, we thank you for accountants and calculators and spreadsheets, but teach us where they fit in the sequence of your kingdom and your will. We believe that your vision done in your way always leads to your provision. Come, Holy Spirit, and deliver us from our easy assumption that our conventional ways and methodologies are your ways. Trumpets, Lord. Thank you for reminding us that you defeat armies and bring down walls with trumpets. For yours is the kingdom and the power and the glory, Lord Jesus. Yours alone. In Jesus' name we pray, amen.

The Questions

- Do you tend to say yes before the Lord gives a vision or assignment, or do you tend to need more data before saying yes? What might preemptive obedience mean to you?

The Problem with Grasshoppers and Giants

23

NUMBERS 13:30–33 | Then Caleb silenced the people before Moses and said, "We should go up and take possession of the land, for we can certainly do it."

But the men who had gone up with him said, "We can't attack those people; they are stronger than we are." And they spread among the Israelites a bad report about the land they had explored. They said, "The land we explored devours those living in it. All the people we saw there are of great size. We saw the Nephilim there (the descendants of Anak come from the Nephilim). We seemed like grasshoppers in our own eyes, and we looked the same to them."

Consider This

Minority report: We should go up and take possession of the land, for we can certainly do it.

Majority report: We can't attack those people. They are stronger than we are. The land devours those living in it. All the people are of great size. We saw the Nephilim. We seemed like grasshoppers in our own eyes. We seemed like grasshoppers in their eyes too.

Verse 33 is where it always goes south: "We saw the Nephilim there (the descendants of Anak come from the Nephilim). We seemed like grasshoppers in our own eyes, and we looked the same to them."

We gaze upon the opponent. We compare ourselves to the opponent. We assume the opponent sees us the way we see ourselves. What's missing here? God. In fact, we don't see any expression of faith in God in this entire exchange today. Caleb seems to have a lot of self-confidence, noting we should because we can. It comes off a bit like overconfidence. The others seem afraid and quite under-confident. Under-confidence, however, is not humility. It is fear.

The big issue is whose eyes are on God. When our eyes are not on God, they are on ourselves. When our eyes are on ourselves, we then compare ourselves to others. Faith focuses, even fixates, on God—who God is, what God has done, and what God can do. When we see God truly, we see ourselves in reality. If we aren't beholding our God, we are destined to see ourselves and others in the framework of grasshoppers and giants, constantly switching roles based on the ephemerality of our own confidence or lack thereof.

This is why the Word of God is so critically important. And we don't want to read it with ourselves in the middle of the frame but with God in the center. We must learn to read with the primary matter in view—what is God like and what can God do? How does this apply to my life and what do I need to do is, at best, a secondary question and often a tertiary one.

Unfortunately, we have tended to make this the main point. It has led us into a highly functional faith focused on our capacities and activities (or lack thereof). What we must develop is a more contemplative faith trained to behold a dynamically transcendent God who delights in the lack of human capacity and the frailty of human activity because his strength is made perfect in our weakness.

The word of encouragement to anyone facing challenging scenarios or difficult circumstances is not "You can do it." The word of encouragement is "Behold, our God."

The Prayer

Father, save us from looking in the mirror. Let us instead lift our eyes to the hills and ask from where does our help come? Our help comes from the Lord, the maker of heaven and earth. Come, Holy Spirit, and deliver us from our thin frameworks of faith, which subtly center on ourselves, our capacities, and our abilities, or the lack thereof. Lead us into a faith wholly consumed with God alone. In Jesus' name we pray, amen.

The Questions

- Are you grasping this contrast between a highly functional faith that centers on our capacities and abilities and a contemplative faith in a transcendent God? How would you say what I am struggling to say?

Encouragement Is Not the Cure for Discouragement but the Immunization

24

NUMBERS 14:1–5 | That night all the members of the community raised their voices and wept aloud. All the Israelites grumbled against Moses and Aaron, and the whole assembly said to them, "If only we had died in Egypt! Or in this wilderness! Why is the LORD bringing us to this land only to let us fall by the sword? Our wives and children will be taken as plunder. Wouldn't it be better for us to go back to Egypt?" And they said to each other, "We should choose a leader and go back to Egypt."

Then Moses and Aaron fell facedown in front of the whole Israelite assembly gathered there.

Consider This

It's interesting to note the difference between discouragement and encouragement. Discouragement is like a contagious disease. Note, however, encouragement is not a cure. Encouragement is more like an immunization. Diseases spread without effort. Immunizations must be administered one person at a time.

As the two reports of the twelve spies settle over the camp, the diseased contagion of discouragement has landed on the people of God. It has spread through them like a plague. The text is careful to tell us that "all the members of the community raised their voices and wept aloud" and that "all the Israelites grumbled against Moses and Aaron."

Discouragement produces despair: *If only we had died in Egypt! Or in this wilderness!*

Discouragement produces self-pity: *Why is the Lord bringing us to this land only to let us fall by the sword?*

Discouragement produces a preemptive spirit of defeat: *Our wives and children will be taken as plunder.*

Discouragement produces retreat: *Wouldn't it be better for us to go back to Egypt?*

Discouragement produces dissension and mutiny: *And they said to each other, "We should choose a leader and go back to Egypt."*

Did you notice what is missing from today's text? Faith in God. When people get discouraged, they don't deal with God. They attack their leaders. This is why anyone attempting to live a life of faith and obedience and even remotely pursue an assignment or calling from God must be encouraged.

Rehearsing now: encouragement is not the cure but the immunization. Without the ongoing, daily immunization of encouragement, we are susceptible to the contagion of discouragement. Discouragement leads us into the deception of sin and onward into the condition known as hardness of heart. So if encouragement is not the cure for discouragement, what then is the cure? I believe it is empathy. It is to come alongside a person who suffers from discouragement and enter into it with them, not attempting to correct it or solve it but to feel it and to some degree absorb it. It is to enter into the darkness with them.

Perhaps I'm stretching here, but I see some measure of this in Moses and Aaron's response to the angry, hard-hearted people in verse 5:

Then Moses and Aaron fell facedown in front of the whole Israelite assembly gathered there.

They were clearly taking on the posture of intercessors here, standing between the people and God, preparing to intercede. Intercession requires empathy—deep identification with the pain of another. Empathy requires humility—leaving behind one's own point of view and frame of reference in order to enter into that of another. They were not preparing to make a noble speech of encouragement. They were preparing to deal with God.

There is a lot here to reflect on and ponder. Let's give ourselves to such work today, asking Jesus to reveal himself to us through this scene and to tutor us in the unlikely way of the cross unfolding.

The Prayer

Father, we perceive great pain in today's text, great discouragement, deepening empathy, and even compassion in the face of stinging criticism. We perceive the profound mystery of the cross here. Lord Jesus, show us where you are in this text. Come, Holy Spirit, and give us the spirit of wisdom and revelation that we may know Jesus better. In his name we pray, amen.

The Questions

· What do you make of this notion of encouragement as immunization against the disease of discouragement and empathy as the cure once discouragement takes hold of someone? Encouragement is meant to prevent discouragement more than it is to respond to it. Make sense? Have you ever tried to talk someone out of their discouragement?

How Encouragers Win Even When They Lose

25

NUMBERS 14:5–9 | Then Moses and Aaron fell facedown in front of the whole Israelite assembly gathered there. Joshua son of Nun and Caleb son of Jephunneh, who were among those who had explored the land, tore their clothes and said to the entire Israelite assembly, "The land we passed through and explored is exceedingly good. If the LORD is pleased with us, he will lead us into that land, a land flowing with milk and honey, and will give it to us. Only do not rebel against the LORD. And do not be afraid of the people of the land, because we will devour them. Their protection is gone, but the LORD is with us. Do not be afraid of them."

Consider This

This meeting has clearly gone off the rails. The people are crying and yelling. They are grumbling and cursing under their breath. In a move of desperate devotion, Moses and Aaron have fallen facedown on the ground in front of the whole assembly. Now Joshua and Caleb, the two members of the minority report, begin ripping their clothes. This meeting is headed for mutiny. Coaches are about to be axed mid-season. This is clearly going to be a major turning point in the story.

The promised land movement is all but lost. Against all odds, Joshua and Caleb determine to express their encouragement to the people, come what may. Let's break their speech down into its enumerated points.

1. The land we passed through and explored is exceedingly good;

2. If the Lord is pleased with us, he will lead us into that land, a land flowing with milk and honey, and will give it to us;

3. Only do not rebel against the Lord;

4. And do not be afraid of the people of the land;

5. We will devour them;

6. Their protection is gone;

7. But the Lord is with us; and

8. Do not be afraid of them.

"The Lord." Did you see how many times they referred to the Lord? Count them. Three times they witness to the presence and power of God.

I love that the designated leaders of the people, Moses and Aaron, are not the ones giving this exhortation. They are facedown on the floor. I love the courage of these two eyewitnesses, leaving everything on the field, knowing the other ten eyewitnesses are not with them. They have taken a courageous stand, knowing they will likely not carry the day.

This is what our ascended Lord Jesus Christ is watching for every minute of every day. He is looking for those whose eyes are fixed on him, who will give witness to the Lord around the family table, in the church council meeting, at the executive committee session at work, from city hall to the halls of Congress. He looks not so much for people to say religious things but to say and do righteous things. He is looking for those whose hearts belong wholly to him.

Why is encouragement so essential? Because discouragement is so dangerous. Discouragement is toxic, like a malignant cancer, spreading a spirit of defeat and despair, which most often leads to division. As we walk through this story, I am beginning to see the strategy and movement of encouragement. It begins with empathy and deep identification with a person or community. Then it moves to a shared remembrance of the story so far. It then moves into a mode of prophetic co-presencing, creating the space for the Holy Spirit to move and minister to the heart of a person or community. This is the space where deep begins to call out to deep, before and even beyond words. The final move is one of exhortation, where our words take on supernatural capacities to freight the heart and mind of God for and into another.

Here's the best part: this story will not end well, but we will never stop talking about Caleb and Joshua. The witness of encouragement always wins, even when it is on a losing team.

The Prayer

Father, teach and train us in this essential work of encouragement. Give us the eyes of Jesus to see others, the deep heart to hear them, the ears to listen for what you are saying over them, the patience to wait on you, and the boldness to speak—come what may. I know it begins with my own wholehearted belonging to you, Jesus. Come, Holy Spirit, and encourage our hearts to this end and these outcomes. In Jesus' name we pray, amen.

The Questions

- How is this approach and framework for encouragement encouraging you? Challenging you? How will you grow in your appropriation of it?

26 Why to Love God Means to Fear God

NUMBERS 14:10–12 | But the whole assembly talked about stoning them. Then the glory of the LORD appeared at the tent of meeting to all the Israelites. The LORD said to Moses, "How long will these people treat me with contempt? How long will they refuse to believe in me, in spite of all the signs I have performed among them? I will strike them down with a plague and destroy them, but I will make you into a nation greater and stronger than they."

Consider This

Recovering our place in this meeting that just won't end, Caleb has just taken his seat after giving the Braveheart speech of his life. *Maybe, just maybe*, he might have thought to himself, *they will rise up and call me blessed and line up to take the hill*. If so, he could not have been more wrong. Look what happened next:

But the whole assembly talked about stoning them.

"Them," in this case, were Joshua and Caleb (a.k.a. the minority report). Does the phrase "Blessed are those who are persecuted because of righteousness" (Matt. 5:10) ring a bell? Thank you, Jesus.

Now the drama goes next level. Get a load of this:

Then the glory of the LORD appeared at the tent of meeting to all the Israelites.

This can't be good. I think of the glory of the Lord like a flaming diamond with infinite facets. The particular facet one sees depends on the moment they face. It could be a calming whisper, as in Elijah's case. It could be a blazing chariot, as also in Elijah's case. No matter the particular moment and mode of manifestation, one thing holds true—one must never assume, presume, or in any way become familiar with the glorious presence of the Lord.

There is an old saying that seems apropos for today's text: familiarity breeds contempt. The closer we come to power, the more familiar we tend to become with it and the more contempt we tend to develop for it, especially if we think we have power and our power is somehow being called into question or offended. This is the prideful nature of the human heart. This is where hardness of heart comes from. These people had become familiar with God. Hear the Word of God in this light:

The Lord said to Moses, "How long will these people treat me with contempt? How long will they refuse to believe in me, in spite of all the signs I have performed among them?"

In case anyone was wondering, this meeting is not going well, nor is it going to end happily.

"I will strike them down with a plague and destroy them, but I will make you into a nation greater and stronger than they."

We humans have a tendency to want to be cozy with the God of the universe. Because we are family, we trend toward familiarity, and we know where familiarity leads: contempt. No matter how long we walk with God, no matter how far we have come, the minute we begin to lose the holy awe and fear of God, we need to cover our faces, rend our hearts, and hit the floor. In fact, this familiarity that unwittingly trends toward the presumption of mercy and even grace is the sign that our hearts have become hardened and sin has, in fact, deceived us. It is a perilous place. The sign of walking closely with Jesus is that though we know we have everything in him, we take nothing for granted from him. He will be our friend but not our "little buddy."

The letter to the Hebrews opens with the word on encouragement, but I want to show you where it closes. It is not a pleasant text, but one we must heed, for we are people of the whole counsel of God.

> If we deliberately keep on sinning after we have received the knowledge of the truth, no sacrifice for sins is left, but only a fearful expectation of judgment and of raging fire that will consume the enemies of God. Anyone who rejected the law of Moses died without mercy on the testimony of two or three witnesses. How much more severely do you think someone deserves to be punished who has trampled the Son of God underfoot, who has treated as an unholy thing the blood of the covenant that sanctified them, and who has insulted the Spirit of grace? For we know him who said, "It is mine to avenge; I will repay," and again, "The Lord will judge his people." It is a dreadful thing to fall into the hands of the living God. (10:26–31)

> Therefore, since we are receiving a kingdom that cannot be shaken, let us be thankful, and so worship God acceptably with reverence and awe, for our "God is a consuming fire." (Heb. 12:28–29)

The Prayer
Father, thank you for letting us call you "Father," and yet thank you for reminding us that you are the almighty God

of the cosmos, the maker of heaven and earth, the Lord, the King of the universe. We stand in awe of you. We bow in trembling fear before you. And we live in holy love for you. Forgive us for our familiarity, our casual ways of approaching you. And yet thank you, Jesus, for being our friend like no other. Come, Holy Spirit, and train our hearts to walk well with you in this world. In Jesus' name, amen.

The Question

- So where do you locate yourself these days on the spectrum:
  Casual Familiarity ——————— Holy Awe, Fear, and Love

27 For His Name's Sake

NUMBERS 14:13–16 | Moses said to the LORD, "Then the Egyptians will hear about it! By your power you brought these people up from among them. And they will tell the inhabitants of this land about it. They have already heard that you, LORD, are with these people and that you, LORD, have been seen face to face, that your cloud stays over them, and that you go before them in a pillar of cloud by day and a pillar of fire by night. If you put all these people to death, leaving none alive, the nations who have heard this report about you will say, 'The LORD was not able to bring these people into the land he promised them on oath, so he slaughtered them in the wilderness.'"

Consider This

Let's begin by remembering the last thing God said to Moses in yesterday's text: "I will strike them down with a plague and destroy them, but I will make you into a nation greater and stronger than they" (v. 12).

Moses does a fascinating thing here—and in quite subversively, lawyerly manner. He doesn't defend the people. He appeals to the honorable reputation of the Judge.

"If you put all these people to death, leaving none alive, the nations who have heard this report about you will say, 'The Lord was not able to bring these people into the land he promised them on oath, so he slaughtered them in the wilderness.'"

Moses' client (a.k.a. the people of Israel) have given him no leg to stand on. They are guilty as charged. He is not appealing for mercy or even one more chance—just yet. He is not throwing himself on the mercy of the court. No, Moses is appealing to the glorious reputation of God.

Let me take what will seem like a left turn here. In the mornings, on the way to school over the years, I have tried to claim the time to rehearse key texts of Scripture with my children. Sam is the only one left that I still drive to school, and he turns sixteen next month, so my days are numbered. For his eighth-grade year, we rehearsed Psalm 23 every single morning—okay, most of them. For his ninth-grade year, we did Psalm 24. We are working on Matthew 5:1–10 (the Beatitudes) now. I will say one verse, and he will say the next and so on. Sam makes an error, almost habitually, every single time we do Psalm 23. Here's how it goes:

Dad: The Lord is my Shepherd . . .

Sam: I shall not want . . .

Dad: He makes me lie down in green pastures . . .

Sam: For his name's sake . . .

Dad: He leads me beside still waters . . .

Sam: For his name's sake . . .

Dad: He leads me in paths of righteousness . . .

Sam: For his name's sake . . .

"Finally!" I want to say. "For his name's sake" comes after "he leads me in paths of righteousness, Sam!" And yesterday, it finally hit me. Sam is exactly right. "For his name's sake" comes after everything he does! Thank you, Sam!

This is what Moses was getting at in today's text:

"If you put all these people to death, leaving none alive, the nations who have heard this report about you will say, 'The LORD was not able to bring these people into the land he promised them on oath, so he slaughtered them in the wilderness.'"

For his name's sake! Anything and everything God does is done for his name's sake. And here's the amazing grace part: when his name is exalted, it is simultaneously and irrevocably for his glory, for our gain, and for others' good.

So, yes, Lord. Hallowed be your name! For your name's sake! All the time!

The Prayer

Our Father, for your name's sake we live and move and have our being. Make it more so today than it was yesterday. Lord Jesus, yours is the name that is above every name.

Mountains bow down and the sea will roar at the sound of your name! Thank you for naming us "Christian," a name after your own name. Come, Holy Spirit, and write the name of love and holiness on our hearts, that our lives would be lived for your name's sake. Yes, Lord, this is my aspiration and ambition. In Jesus' name, amen.

The Question

- "For his name's sake." Write these words in different places today throughout your day—in your journal, on the top of the next meeting agenda, on the napkin at lunch, on a sticky note in the car, on the mirror in your bathroom, on the back of the door on the way outside. "For his name's sake."

The Love of God and the Love of Moses

28

NUMBERS 14:17–19 | "Now may the Lord's strength be displayed, just as you have declared: 'The Lord is slow to anger, abounding in love and forgiving sin and rebellion. Yet he does not leave the guilty unpunished; he punishes the children for the sin of the parents to the third and fourth generation.' In accordance with your great love, forgive the sin of these people, just as you have pardoned them from the time they left Egypt until now."

Consider This

Moses really is something else. He appeals to God for God's own name's sake. Now he reminds God of God's own identity and character.

"The Lord is slow to anger, abounding in love and forgiving sin and rebellion. Yet he does not leave the guilty unpunished; he punishes the children for the sin of the parents to the third and fourth generation."

Moses now moves from lawyer to intercessor and priest.

"In accordance with your great love, forgive the sin of these people, just as you have pardoned them from the time they left Egypt until now."

Bottom line: Moses loves God and God's people with a God-like love. He had every reason to be done with them. They have complained about him, grumbled at him, threatened to leave him, and acted like complete idiotic, imbecilic children over and over again. Still, Moses has gone back to bat for them over and over again. God even gave Moses a massive exit strategy, saying, "I will strike them down with a plague and destroy them, but I will make you into a nation greater and stronger than they" (Num. 14:12).

You know why Moses didn't give up on these people? Because he remembered God never gave up on him. God is ever searching for people who will not give up on his people—men and women who have the stick-to-it tenacity to take the long, winding wilderness path of learning to love people like God loves people.

As we will soon see, this is going to cost Moses not only another forty years in the wilderness with this bunch but also his chance to ever set foot in the promised land.

This is earth-shaking, breathtaking love, friends—legendary love. Be encouraged, saints! God loves nothing more than to land this kind of love in the lives of ordinary people.

The Prayer

Father, our capacity to love is so limited. Your capacity to love is never-ending. How do we learn to love like you love? We want to become the kind of person who does not give up on other people. We want to be like Jesus. Thank you for Jesus. Jesus, I belong to you. Come, Holy Spirit, and help us learn to behold Jesus in such a way that you can make us like him. In his name we pray, amen.

The Question

• What do you learn about loving God and loving people from Moses in today's text?

On Having a Different Spirit

29

NUMBERS 14:20–25 | The LORD replied, "I have forgiven them, as you asked. Nevertheless, as surely as I live and as surely as the glory of the Lord fills the whole earth, not one of those who saw my glory and the signs I performed in Egypt and in the wilderness but who disobeyed me and tested me ten times—not one of them will ever see the land I promised on oath to their ancestors. No one who has treated me with contempt will ever see it. But because my servant Caleb has a different spirit and follows me wholeheartedly, I will bring him into the land he went to, and his descendants will inherit it. Since the Amalekites and the Canaanites are living in the valleys, turn back tomorrow and set out toward the desert along the route to the Red Sea."

Consider This

About twenty-five years ago I made a new friend who introduced me to today's text. He and I began working at a church in The Woodlands, Texas, on the same day. Though we were quite different people, we had a lot in common—both from small towns, both fans of country music, and both lovers of Jesus. We first met in the break room of this church we had come to serve. We learned in that encounter that we were both there to help our mutual friend, Bob Swan, begin what would become a profound community of faith within The Woodlands Methodist Church called the Harvest. As we shook hands, I said, "I'm John David Walt." He replied, "I'm Chris Tomlin."

I should tell you, this was before he really became "Chris Tomlin," whose songs would go on to become more than a few of the most-sung songs in the world in the last hundred years. I introduced him to our New Room Conference a couple years back, saying, "This guy would go on to become Chris Tomlin, and I am still John David Walt."

So why am I telling you this? After all, Billy Graham once told me to never drop names. I bring it up because soon after we met, we found ourselves talking about the texts and verses of Scripture that had meant the most to us. I have no memory of what I shared, but I will never forget his. He said his life verse was Numbers 14:24.

"But because my servant Caleb has a different spirit and follows me wholeheartedly, I will bring him into the land he went to, and his descendants will inherit it."

It takes a person of a different spirit to even claim Numbers 14:24 as a life verse, doesn't it? At that point in my life and faith, the book of Numbers hadn't exactly been one of my go-to books for inspiration. I'll credit Chris, who remains a close friend to this day (lives about two miles from me now) for this stretch, now going on two weeks, through Numbers 13–14.

"But because my servant Caleb has a different spirit and follows me wholeheartedly, I will bring him into the land he went to, and his descendants will inherit it."

Behind this word *spirit* is the Hebrew word *ruach*. It is the exact same term we see in Genesis 1:2: "The Spirit of God was hovering over the waters." It's the same concept we see in Acts 2:2 where it says, "Suddenly a sound like the blowing of a violent wind came from heaven and filled the whole house where they were sitting." And behind this word *wholeheartedly*, we see the Hebrew term pronounced "maw-lay," which means "to be filled or full." It's the same term we see in Exodus 40, where "the glory of the Lᴏʀᴅ filled the tabernacle."

"But because my servant Caleb has a different spirit and follows me wholeheartedly . . ."

Here's my amateur translation: Caleb has set his sail to catch the wind of Holy Spirit and the vessel of his heart is filled with the fullness of God.

If you are reading this book, it's because you have a different spirit and aspire to follow Jesus wholeheartedly. You are part of the minority report. You stand in the line of Caleb and Joshua. I am writing to people whose hearts beat to the tune of Numbers 14:24.

"But because my servant Caleb has a different spirit and follows me wholeheartedly, I will bring him into the land he went to, and his descendants will inherit it."

The Prayer

Father, thank you for giving us a different spirit, one that causes us to follow you wholeheartedly. Jesus, we belong to you—with our whole hearts. Come, Holy Spirit, and make it more and more and more so every single day. Thank you for encouraging us. In Jesus' name we pray, amen.

The Questions

- Does Numbers 14:24 fit for you? Are you growing in this different spirit to follow Jesus wholeheartedly?

On Faithfulness, Failure, Forgiveness, and the Fallout

30

NUMBERS 14:26–35 | The LORD said to Moses and Aaron: "How long will this wicked community grumble against me? I have heard the complaints of these grumbling Israelites. So tell them, 'As surely as I live, declares the LORD, I will do to you the very thing I heard you say: In this wilderness your bodies will fall—every one of you twenty years old or more who was counted in the census and who has grumbled against me. Not one of you will enter the land I swore with uplifted hand to make your home, except Caleb son of Jephunneh and Joshua son of Nun. As for your children that you said would be taken as plunder, I will bring them in to enjoy the land you have rejected. But as for you, your bodies will fall in this wilderness. Your children will be shepherds here for forty years, suffering for your unfaithfulness, until the last of your bodies lies in the wilderness. For forty years—one year for each of the forty days you explored the land—you will suffer for your sins and know what it is like to have me against you.' I, the LORD, have spoken, and I will surely do these things to this whole wicked community, which has banded together against me. They will meet their end in this wilderness; here they will die."

Consider This

Faithfulness. If there is anything we can say about God in his relationship with his people, it is this: God has been faithful. God's grace had been beyond extraordinary for these former slaves. He delivered them from slavery, walked them out of the country, parted the Red Sea, destroyed Pharaoh's army, led them by day and night through the wilderness, fed them morning and evening, entered into covenant with them to be their God, promised them a land flowing with milk and honey, and on we could go. God had been faithful.

Failure. God's people failed. But who is keeping score, right? Apparently, God is. It's interesting how God says that they "disobeyed me and tested me ten times" (Num. 14:22). (I wonder about the correlation between this and the ten plagues by which God tested Pharaoh.) But didn't Paul say that love "keeps no record of wrongs" (1 Cor. 13:5)? And what happened to God casting our sins into the sea of forgetfulness and remembering them no more (Mic. 7:19)? It's a good question.

Let's recall Moses' prayer again: "In accordance with your great love, forgive the sin of these people, just as you have pardoned them from the time they left Egypt until now" (Num. 14:19).

God forgave and forgave and forgave to the tenth power. Every act of forgiveness offered an opportunity for the people to bear the fruit of repentance. Instead, they did the opposite and presumed on grace. I recall a situation in my own life in a difficult relationship where I forgave and forgave and forgave and hit reset time after time after time. From my perspective, each time it was like the transgression never happened. It was forgotten. Finally, there came a point in the relationship where I could forgive, but I could no longer hit reset. This is the point where all the forgiven debts come back on the ledger, not so forgiveness can somehow be retracted but so mercy can be reframed. There comes a point in a persistent pattern of broken behavior where the deeper condition must be identified for a different kind of intervention. There is a word for this deeper condition in these seeming intractable situations: *contempt*. There is a point at which persistent trespassing must be called out for what it is—contempt toward the one who has been repeatedly trespassed against.

It's interesting how the Hebrew word (pronounced "nawats") behind the translated English word *contempt* means "to blaspheme." Contempt comes from a place of crystallized disrespect. Contempt is a hallmark expression of a hardened heart. Contempt can be forgiven, and it must be. It just can't be tolerated. This is the place where reset no longer works and, in fact, becomes dangerous and even irresponsible. This is the place where sin's consequences must be allowed to run their course. This is the place where failure must finally be allowed to face and feel the fallout. That is exactly what happened here:

"But as for you, your bodies will fall in this wilderness. Your children will be shepherds here for forty years, suffering for your unfaithfulness, until the last of your bodies lies in the wilderness. For forty years—one year for each of the forty days you explored the land—you will suffer for your sins and know what

*it is like to have me against you.' I, the LORD, have spoken, and
I will surely do these things to this whole wicked community,
which has banded together against me. They will meet their
end in this wilderness; here they will die."*

This is quite sobering, isn't it? You likely see many analogies across the past and present relational landscape of your life. This is why the stakes are so high when it comes to encouragement. It takes a while to reach hardness of heart, and it comes through the subtle deceitfulness of sin. "But encourage one another daily, as long as it is called "Today," so that none of you may be hardened by sin's deceitfulness" (Heb. 3:13).

The Prayer

Father, thank you for your long-suffering, patient, merciful, grace-filled, slow-to-anger way with us. We want our hearts to be laid bare before you. Have we or are we presuming on your grace? Are the seeds of contempt sown in our hearts toward you? Toward others? Come, Holy Spirit, and reveal to us the connection between contempt for others and contempt for you. Reveal our own propensity to be deceived at just this point. Create in us clean hearts and renew a right spirit within us. We pray in Jesus' name, amen.

The Questions

- How do you relate to this concept of contempt? Where have you seen it in others? In your relationships? In yourself?

Why Discouragement Means Death

31

NUMBERS 14:36–38 | So the men Moses had sent to explore the land, who returned and made the whole community grumble against him by spreading a bad report about it—these men who were responsible for spreading the bad report about the land were struck down and died of a plague before the Lord. Of the men who went to explore the land, only Joshua son of Nun and Caleb son of Jephunneh survived.

Consider This

We come to a very hard teaching today.

So the men Moses had sent to explore the land, who returned and made the whole community grumble against him by spreading a bad report about it—these men who were responsible for spreading the bad report about the land were struck down and died of a plague before the Lord.

Something in me doesn't want God to be this way. I mean, couldn't we just demote them or dock their pay or fire them? Why death? This is the Word of God, however, and I don't sit in judgment on this Word. I sit under its judgment. So I ask, "What would you teach me here, Lord?" Here is what I am hearing and seeing in this text: our words carry great weight. Words create worlds, and they can also destroy them. Listen to the brother of Jesus on this point:

> When we put bits into the mouths of horses to make them obey us, we can turn the whole animal. Or take ships as an example. Although they are so large and are driven by strong winds, they are steered by a very small rudder wherever the pilot wants to go. Likewise, the tongue is a small part of the body, but it makes great boasts. Consider what a great forest is set on fire by a small spark. The tongue also is a fire, a world of evil among the parts of the body. It corrupts the whole body, sets the whole course of one's life on fire, and is itself set on fire by hell. (James 3:3–6)

Many of you reading this do not have an adequate grasp on the power of your words. It is the single greatest power you have to steward. The highest stewardship you can exercise with your words is the choice to be an encourager. Don't confuse this with positive-thinking optimism. And don't mistake this to mean encouragers don't say hard things when needed. Whether challenging or inspiring, the task of an encourager is to speak the truth in love so that "we will grow to become in every respect the mature body of him who is the head, that is, Christ" (Eph. 4:15).

The most damaging and devastating thing we can do with our words is to discourage others. Look at the destructive fire started by the words of the ten spies (a.k.a. the majority report). It spread through the people like a forest fire, scorching faith and burning hope to the ground. Look at the extraordinary cost of this cancer of discouragement: forty years of wandering, lostness, and more funerals than we can count.

Here's the real tragedy: the God of heaven and earth was not asking these twelve spies for their opinion on his Word and promise. He was not calling for the question. This was never meant to be an up or down vote on the Word of God. We do not sit in judgment on the Word of God. We stand under God's authority as we humbly seek to understand his will in all things. Encouragement—and consequently discouragement—is a matter of life and death. Encouragement is life. Discouragement is death.

I love this opening declaration in the Sower's Creed: Today, I stake everything on the promise of the Word of God. (You can find the full Sower's Creed on the last page of this book.)

The Prayer

Father, we declare it: Today, we stake everything on the promise of the Word of God. Thank you that your Word is your promise, and your promise is everything. Train our words after your words. Teach us to say what you say and to do what you do and to think like you think. Awaken us to the power of our words to encourage. Come, Holy Spirit, and train us to always speak the truth in love so that others might flourish. We pray in Jesus' name, amen.

The Questions

- Do you tend to think to yourself, *What difference can my words make? Do my words even matter? Does anyone even listen to me?* If so, why do you think you tend to think this way? What will it take to wake up to the truth?

Broken Heart to Hardened Heart to Broken Heart to Healed Heart

32

NUMBERS 14:39–43 | When Moses reported this to all the Israelites, they mourned bitterly. Early the next morning they set out for the highest point in the hill country, saying, "Now we are ready to go up to the land the LORD promised. Surely we have sinned!"

But Moses said, "Why are you disobeying the LORD's command? This will not succeed! Do not go up, because the LORD is not with you. You will be defeated by your enemies, for the Amalekites and the Canaanites will face you there. Because you have turned away from the LORD, he will not be with you and you will fall by the sword."

Consider This

It should not be lost on us that the whole context of our banner text—Hebrews 3:13—is the wilderness world of the people of God: "But encourage one another daily, as long as it is called 'Today,' so that none of you may be hardened by sin's deceitfulness."

Who were they who heard and rebelled? Were they not all those Moses led out of Egypt? And with whom was he angry for forty years? Was it not with those who sinned, whose bodies perished in the wilderness? And to whom did God swear that they would never enter his rest if not to those who disobeyed? So we see that they were not able to enter, because of their unbelief. (Heb. 3:16–19)

Here's the encouragement to some of you today. Doors have closed in your life because of your disobedience—some of them permanently. But the story is not done. A new door presents itself. Jesus stands at that door and knocks. He wants to come in and meet with you in a new way, for a new season, for new purposes he wants to unfold in your life. He wants to heal your heart of the hardness. Only he can. No one willfully hardens their heart. They do it because sin deceives them into doing it. You see, a hard heart comes from a broken heart. Some situation or circumstance or relational dysfunction or trauma has broken your heart. You turned to all the wrong places. It resulted in your heart hardening over time, and now you find yourself in a wilderness of wandering.

I want you to notice, though, the impulse of the hardened heart in response to a closed door.

They mourned bitterly . . .

So far, so good. But it looks like they were sad about the consequences and not the condition of their hearts.

Early the next morning they set out for the highest point in the hill country, saying, "Now we are ready to go up to the land the Lord promised."

Then this: *"Surely we have sinned!"* Note how this is hardly a confession. This is how a hardened heart deals with fault. They keep it super fuzzy. There may be a hint of admission but nowhere near true confession.

It's kind of like saying you are sorry or trying to make amends at gunpoint or after the guilty verdict—as an effort to avoid the consequences. It doesn't work that way. Hear Moses' response:

But Moses said, "Why are you disobeying the Lord's command? This will not succeed! Do not go up, because the Lord is not with you. You will be defeated by your enemies, for the Amalekites and the Canaanites will face you there. Because you have turned away from the Lord, he will not be with you and you will fall by the sword."

There is only one appropriate, effective, and redemptive response for a person who has turned away from the Lord: turning back to the Lord—returning to the Lord—with all your heart. This is the new door, the open door, the door to the future, and it leads into a new room of healing, restoration, and wholehearted repentance—which is the comprehensive realignment of one's life with the will and ways of Jesus. Just as a broken heart becomes a hardened heart, so a hardened heart must become a broken heart again. This is the way to the healed, whole, and holy heart. There is the heartbreak that leads to hardness and the heartbreak that leads to healing.

I sense I am talking to a lot of people today. Jesus is showing you the calcified and calloused places in your heart. He is showing you the symptoms of a critical spirit and a defensive posture and how the subtle and not-so-subtle dispositions of malcontentedness and contempt have set up shop in your spirit like malware on a computer. For some of you, these darkened ways seem to have taken you over. You literally can't fix it, and you are so weary of trying to put a good face on it. It is so draining to live this way.

Be encouraged. Jesus can heal your heart beyond your imagining. You must give him complete access. The door only opens from your side. Locate yourself before him today. Declare the open door. Invite the Holy Spirit to begin the cleanse, to apply the salve, to order the new season of new creation.

This is not the time to try to take the hill. It is the season for the healing of the heart.

The Prayer

Father, we declare it: the doors of our hearts are open to the healing balm of Jesus. In fact, we are going to take them off the hinges. We are weary of trying to change our behavior while keeping the doors to our hearts closed. You have full and complete access. We will wait on you. You are the Lord our healer. Lead us in every way you see fit to help us— through wise counselors, to a band of brothers or sisters, to a pastor or shepherd friend, by your sovereign Word and Spirit. Yes, come, Holy Spirit, and re-break our broken and hardened hearts for your name's sake, for our good, for others' gain. We pray in Jesus' name, amen.

The Question

- Do you struggle with a tendency to criticize others, to complain about situations, to be defensive about yourself, to withdraw from others when you feel offended? If so, these are all signs of a wounded heart. Jesus heals but you must open the door to him. It will take time, but it will be so worth it. Don't wander in the wilderness another year, or another day.

33 Why We Must Stop Trying to Take the Hill

NUMBERS 14:44–45 | Nevertheless, in their presumption they went up toward the highest point in the hill country, though neither Moses nor the ark of the LORD's covenant moved from the camp. Then the Amalekites and the Canaanites who lived in that hill country came down and attacked them and beat them down all the way to Hormah.

Consider This

The three most devastating words in today's text: "in their presumption."

The Hebrew term there is pronounced "aw-fal." It means literally "to swell." It denotes a kind of willfulness born of pride, self-confidence, and determination to go one's own way. The word *stubborn* comes to mind. On an earlier occasion, God used the term *stiff-necked* to describe these people. It comes from the image of an ox that will not respond to commands or goading but bears down and goes its own direction anyway. For all its strength, it is useless. Clearly, I am describing someone you know. They are perhaps living in your home right now.

Strong-willed, controlling people can get a lot done and often accomplish much, but they tend to be an impediment to the Lord. The will of God must be done in the way of God, or it will not be done at all. Today's text is a powerful example. God made his will known to the people that his promise was for them to inhabit the land. They rebelled against his promise. He responded with new guidance. They went against his guidance. They met with failure. One simply cannot do the will of God while disregarding the Word of God, for only the Word of God brings us to understand the ways of God.

> I will instruct you and teach you in the way you
>> should go;
> I will counsel you with my loving eye on you.
> Do not be like the horse or the mule,
>> which have no understanding
> but must be controlled by bit and bridle
> or they will not come to you. (Ps. 32:8–9)

What kind of heart would the Lord fashion in us? The word is *meekness*. "Blessed are the meek, for they will inherit the earth," Jesus teaches (Matt. 5:7). The Bible describes Moses as follows: "Now the man Moses was very meek, more than all people who were on the face of the earth" (Num. 12:3 ESV). A meek person is not a weak person but one who has come to the deep conviction that all of their strength is as weakness to the Lord. They have come to understand that the Lord has no need of their strength, only their surrender. The world trains us to focus on our strengths. Jesus wants us to learn to glory in our weakness. Unbroken strength is an impediment to the work of God. Meekness is broken strength in humbly surrendered reserve. Think of a horse that has been broken so that it might be ridden. An unbroken horse is the essence of meekness. The broken horse still has all the incredible strength, but it is now power in reserve; strength in submission to the guidance and direction of the rider. This is what meekness means. Think also of Jesus, the Son of God, the second person of the Trinity hidden in the humble frame of a Galilean peasant.

Be encouraged, Jesus is our Great Shepherd. He delights in leading us at every turn and in every step, if we would only learn to walk with him. Hear his voice today, saying: "I will instruct you and teach you in the way you should go; I will counsel you with my loving eye on you" (Ps. 32:8).

Cast off your willful, stubborn, self-reliant, independent spirit. That's not who you really are. It is how you (or someone else) thought you needed to be to make it this far. Bless your old self for the gifts and goods it has given and gently lay it aside. You are being made new. What got you here cannot take you to where Jesus is leading.

And there's a "meddling" word in here for Christian Americans in this age of great confusion. Renounce presumption. Stop trying to take the hill. Jesus took the only hill that matters—Calvary. He calls us to bear the cross in the Valley of Vision. Silence the tidal waves of discouragement coming through what parades as today's news. Cast aside your outrage. Put on love. Become meek. Great awakening will depend on it. Or must we wait again for everyone over twenty or thirty to perish in this wilderness? "Wake up, sleeper, rise from the dead, and Christ will shine on you" (Eph. 5:14).

The Prayer

Father, we renounce presumption. We want to run away from any semblance of it. We now run with the abandonment of a trusting child into your grace, goodness, and glory. Jesus, we belong to you. Jesus, we follow you. Expose our controlling nature as a failure to trust in you. Expose our willful disposition as a failure to walk in your ways. Come, Holy Spirit, and train us in the ways of meekness. Show us why we resist. Melt us. Mold us. Fill us. Use us. We pray in Jesus' name, amen.

The Questions

- Are you aware of the voices of discouragement berating you through all manner of media these days? Do you realize the toxic effect it is having on your faith? If you aren't willing to silence it, will you consider giving Jesus twice as much time as you give these voices every day?

34 Why We Must Become Encouragers

HEBREWS 3:7–15 | So, as the Holy Spirit says:

"Today, if you hear his voice,
  do not harden your hearts
as you did in the rebellion,
  during the time of testing in the wilderness,
where your ancestors tested and tried me,
  though for forty years they saw what I did.
That is why I was angry with that generation;
  I said, 'Their hearts are always going astray,
and they have not known my ways.'
  So I declared on oath in my anger,
  'They shall never enter my rest.'"

See to it, brothers and sisters, that none of you has a sinful, unbelieving heart that turns away from the living God. But encourage one another daily, as long as it is called "Today," so that none of you may be hardened by sin's deceitfulness. We have come to share in Christ, if indeed we hold our original conviction firmly to the very end. As has just been said:

"Today, if you hear his voice,
  do not harden your hearts
  as you did in the rebellion."

Consider This

We are somewhere in the middle of a wilderness. "How much longer?" we want to ask. We know we can't turn back. We want to press on, but we are tired and growing weary. This is why encouragement figures so prominently in the lives of those who are following Jesus and seeking his kingdom.

I wanted to revisit our banner text from Hebrews 3 in its entirety. Hebrews is not so much a letter as it is a message. It carries the freight of practically the whole Bible story in the framework of a halftime speech to a winning team who feels like they're losing and wants to quit.

So, as the Holy Spirit says. . .

The Holy Spirit is always speaking, encouraging, comforting, counseling, helping, guiding, warning, bonding, blessing, healing, and doing all the things God does. We see this in full and perfect technicolor display in Jesus of Nazareth, the Messiah. As he was on earth, so he is in heaven, and as he is in heaven, so we are on earth. That's how "on earth as it is in heaven" happens, through his people formed by his Word, filled by his Spirit, being transformed into his own image—for his glory, for our good, for others' gain.

"Today, if you hear his voice . . ."

Here is the big if: *if* you hear his voice. This is where and why encouragement figures so prominently in our lives and faith. One of the everyday ways we can hear the voice of God is through the encouragement of other people. It brings us back to our working definition of encouragement.

To encourage in the biblical sense of the term is to stand in the stead and agency of Jesus, participating in the work of the Holy Spirit, to minister grace to human beings at the level of their inner person, communicating, conveying, and imparting life, love, courage, comfort, consolation, joy, peace, hope, faith, and other dispensations and manifestations of the kingdom of heaven as the moment invites or requires.

". . . do not harden your hearts . . ."

Recall what was written on day 3 about the hardness of heart:

Over the course of our lives, all of us have been through difficult trials. Unjust treatment, unforeseen losses, tragic deaths, life-stealing diseases, betrayals, relationship failures, and all manner of pain and suffering. These things create wilderness seasons that can go on for long periods of time. These are the places where we slowly and often imperceptibly lose faith in God. We would rarely identify it as such, but we begin to shrink back from real trust. We believe in principle but not in an everyday kind of trusting reality. We take on a wilderness wound, and our hearts slowly begin to harden. We don't so much choose hardness as we fail to pursue healing. We allow a wall of protection to be constructed around our heart, and while it does protect us in some ways, it also slowly and imperceptibly isolates us from God and others.

This is how sin deceives us. We mistakenly focus on sin at the level of our behaviors, but our behaviors are merely the symptoms of the sickness. Sin, in its deepest essence, is the condition of an unbelieving heart, and an unbelieving or untrusting heart inevitably becomes a hardened heart. And a hardened heart is the most dangerous place on earth.

"... as you did in the rebellion, during the time of testing in the wilderness."

The wilderness is always a time of testing. The issue is our hearts. Will we harden our hearts or allow them to be hardened? The better question is this: Will we allow our hearts to slowly and subtly shrink back and drift into the realm of unbelief? Recall, it's not that we cease to believe *in* God. We just stop *believing* God. We go to sleep at the wheel of faith.

This is why it says: "See to it, brothers and sisters, that none of you has a sinful, unbelieving heart that turns away from the living God. But encourage one another daily, as long as it is called 'Today,' so that none of you may be hardened by sin's deceitfulness."

Who will you encourage today? Who will encourage you?

The Prayer

Father, we want to pass the wilderness test, and we want to help others pass through it. Would you take our calling to encourage one another to the next level? Come, Holy Spirit, and let us hear your encouraging voice speaking over other people and take the risk to say what we are hearing. We pray in Jesus' name, amen.

The Questions

- Tell an encouragement story that is emerging from this series in your life. Someone you have encouraged? Someone who has encouraged you? What's the story?

35 From A-shakening to Awakening

JOSHUA 1:1–6 | After the death of Moses the servant of the LORD, the LORD said to Joshua son of Nun, Moses' aide: "Moses my servant is dead. Now then, you and all these people, get ready to cross the Jordan River into the land I am about to give to them—to the Israelites. I will give you every place where you set your foot, as I promised Moses. Your territory will extend from the desert to Lebanon, and from the great river, the Euphrates—all the Hittite country—to the Mediterranean Sea in the west. No one will be able to stand against you all the days of your life. As I was with Moses, so I will be with you; I will never leave you nor forsake you. Be strong and courageous, because you will lead these people to inherit the land I swore to their ancestors to give them."

Consider This

We see encouragement everywhere throughout Scripture, but most concentrated in three places: the book of Joshua, the book of the Acts, and the book of Hebrews. We turn today to another massive encouragement text from our story: Joshua.

It had been a long forty years, filled with wandering through the wilderness. The landscape, now littered with tombstones from an entire generation of sin-sick saints, groaned with a tiredness from crying out, "How long, O Lord?"

The page is turning now. The giant Moses has passed on to glory. The curtain lifts and we see Joshua standing at center stage. And mind you, he is not a young man. I'd guess he is somewhere between fifty and seventy, the years when most people these days begin winding down, dreaming about retirement. It had been forty years since he thought he was in his prime, selected for the prestigious SEAL Team Six spy mission into the promised land. He could practically taste the victory, only to be exiled into forty years of wandering in the wilderness—14,600 days of eating manna. He had done most everything right. His heart was all in. Imagine the discouragement and seasons of depression these years brought. It reminds us of his mentor and father in the Lord, Moses, who had such a promising start in Egypt only to find himself exiled to the backside of the wilderness of Midian herding his in-law's sheep for forty years, only to be tapped by God as a sixty-ish year old.

Many people in ministry (heck, in life) begin with visions of grandeur, big dreams, and an indefatigable spirit to take on the world only to meet headlong with the buzzsaw of reality. The move of the Spirit in them gets worn down over time to the tired motions of a sleepy faithfulness. That unholy trifecta of distraction, depression, and discouragement wreaks slow havoc on our souls. Why, God? How long, Lord? This isn't what I signed on for.

It reminds me of Abraham Lincoln, who went through defeat after defeat after defeat in his life and career. At a particularly low point, upon being encouraged to give up and move in a different direction, it is said that Lincoln responded, "I will get ready. My time will come."

Encouragement figures so powerfully in Joshua and Acts because in both of those instances, the people of God were being summoned to wake up and move into the reclamation of the promises of God in their day. The wandering motions of the wilderness were over. The movement was moving again. The day of march was upon them.

"Moses my servant is dead. Now then, you and all these people, get ready to cross the Jordan River into the land I am about to give to them—to the Israelites."

Awakening friends, we must get ready. Our time is coming. Not a day of your past has been wasted. Everything is being gathered up and carried forward into the way ahead. You have not been forgotten or left behind. Get ready. Your time is coming.

Awakening is coming. The global pandemic of COVID-19 was not an awakening. It was what I call "a-shakening." A-shakening can lead to awakening, but it can also lead to another forty years of wandering in the wilderness. The difference? Will we get ready?

"Be strong and courageous, because you will lead these people to inherit the land I swore to their ancestors to give them."

The Prayer

Father, it can be hard to thank you for wilderness wandering at the time. In hindsight, it always seems clear how you were working. Knowing that, we thank you for what you have been and are doing in our hearts, homes, churches, and cities. We believe awakening is coming. We want to be ready. Yes, we will get ready. Come, Holy Spirit, and bring deep awakening to the deepest places in our hearts. Soften our hearts. Show us the hardness. Break up the fallow ground. Declare a season of sowing in our hearts. Melt us. Mold us. Fill us. Use us. In Jesus' name, amen.

The Questions

- How has the wilderness taken it out of you? Are you ready to reconnect the motions of waking up with the movement of awakening?

New Jersey 36

JOSHUA 1:1–6 | After the death of Moses the servant of the LORD, the LORD said to Joshua son of Nun, Moses' aide: "Moses my servant is dead. Now then, you and all these people, get ready to cross the Jordan River into the land I am about to give to them—to the Israelites. I will give you every place where you set your foot, as I promised Moses. Your territory will extend from the desert to Lebanon, and from the great river, the Euphrates—all the Hittite country—to the Mediterranean Sea in the west. No one will be able to stand against you all the days of your life. As I was with Moses, so I will be with you; I will never leave you nor forsake you. Be strong and courageous, because you will lead these people to inherit the land I swore to their ancestors to give them."

Consider This

To live a courageous life, we must make it our daily work to give and receive encouragement. Because we mostly find ourselves in our relatively small context, with our super-limited life—somewhere between a bunker and the front lines of all we are dealing with—one of the big strategies of encouragement is to keep in touch with the big-picture view of things. In order to run and not grow weary and to walk and not faint, we must be regularly lifted up out of the woods of our reality onto the eagle's wings of the Holy Spirit.

Genesis 1 and 2 offer us a picture of the whole creation—the heavens and the earth—as the temple of God with the image-bearers of God created and called to walk with God, be fruitful and multiply, and lead the whole creation toward flourishing abundance. Genesis 3–11 unfold the story of the tragic rebellion and demise of what became a self-serving, God-denying people. Genesis 12 through the rest of the Old Testament is the story of an incredibly small, very focused restart. It is easy to get the picture from reading the Bible, the story of God, that we are talking about something massive and grand. I don't want to burst your bubble, but the majority of the Bible is actually a pretty small story. The plot centers around the promised land, a land flowing with milk and honey, a veritable garden of Eden place. We see its scope in today's text:

"I will give you every place where you set your foot, as I promised Moses. Your territory will extend from the desert to Lebanon, and from the great river, the Euphrates—all the Hittite country—to the Mediterranean Sea in the west."

It always felt so large and grand to me. In truth, this promised land, the focus of most of the Bible and the centerpiece of much of the story, is in actuality roughly the size of the tiny state of New Jersey.

So what's my point here? Am I somehow trying to diminish the story? No, I am attempting to magnify the God. Our God, the God of heaven and earth, the only true and living God, almost always begins very, very, very, very small. Indeed, the God who owns the cattle on a thousand hills, and the hills, chooses to make a promise to one man and engage a relatively small group of people to journey into and inhabit a territory the size of New Jersey. And all told it takes around two thousand years. And it, ultimately, apparently, comes to a disappointing failure with the people expelled from the land and sent into exile because of their persistent hardness of heart and stiff-necked ways.

And it turns out all of this is merely the backstory. For onto this platform of the ruins and rubble of an apparently failed experiment, this God will come himself into his creation, into this little promised land, incarnated in the human flesh of Jesus of Nazareth, the Messiah. This, my friends, is again a very, very, very, very small, incredibly unconventional, unbelievably absurd approach to save the whole world. And look at it now, two thousand years hence, a massive scope and yet still small, seed by seed, one heart at a time.

Friends of the awakening, this is very, very, very, very small, and it is massive—sowing and growing over the entire creation now, billions and billions serving and being served. Take courage. It can actually start with you, your heart, your home, your church, your town—with us.

As we say in the Sower's Creed, "Today, I will remember that the tiniest seeds become the tallest trees." (See the entire Sower's Creed on the last page of this book.)

The Prayer

Father, how can it be? New Jersey! You are so big, and yet you have worked so small. And you have worked so small, and it has become so big. Small, Lord, teach us the small ways, the ways of Jesus. Show us the seed in our hands today, and give us the audacity to sow small and in doing so to sow big. Come, Holy Spirit, and interpret this mystery and this miracle to our deepest hearts and minds. Thank you for sowing this encouragement into us. In Jesus' name, amen.

The Questions

- Are you grasping the mysterious and miraculous nature of the small-big ways of God? How does it encourage you? How will it help you become a better encourager?

His Name Is My Name Too

37

JOSHUA 1:1–6 | After the death of Moses the servant of the LORD, the LORD said to Joshua son of Nun, Moses' aide: "Moses my servant is dead. Now then, you and all these people, get ready to cross the Jordan River into the land I am about to give to them—to the Israelites. I will give you every place where you set your foot, as I promised Moses. Your territory will extend from the desert to Lebanon, and from the great river, the Euphrates—all the Hittite country—to the Mediterranean Sea in the west. No one will be able to stand against you all the days of your life. As I was with Moses, so I will be with you; I will never leave you nor forsake you. Be strong and courageous, because you will lead these people to inherit the land I swore to their ancestors to give them."

Consider This

There is a word of encouragement I have for us today. The word is *agency*. The word *agency* describes the primary way

God works in this world. God, for reasons known only to himself, has chosen to work through the agency of human beings. From Genesis 1 to Revelation 22 and down through all the centuries of world history, God has chosen to work through people like you and me. It seems obvious enough to say, and yet many of us do not adequately grasp this truth and reality. We somehow tend to think God is primarily working outside of human agency, that God is just sort of numinously and mystically working outside of human agency, somehow in the air or atmosphere around and between us.

Think about it. In powerful gatherings of the church, people tend to say, "God really showed up today" or "His presence was thick"—as though God's presence were a substance among us. And we do see precedent for such descriptions, as on Mount Sinai and the dedication of the temple and other occasions. The clear and overwhelming story of the Bible, however, is one of human agency—of human agents endowed with the power and gifts of God to act with his authorization for his glory and the good of others.

Today's text demonstrates this with such clarity in this word from God to Joshua.

1. No one will be able to stand against *you* all the days of your life;

2. As I was with Moses, so I will be with *you*;

3. I will never leave *you* nor forsake *you*;

4. *You* will lead these people to inherit the land I swore to their ancestors to give them; and

5. [Therefore *you*] be strong and courageous.

Encouragement, in the biblical sense of the term, is never "You can do it!" It is always "God will do it." But here's the kicker: God will do it *through you*—not around you, nor because of you, nor in spite of you, nor apart from you, nor just somewhere out there in the air or over the rainbow. No. God will do it through you.

God first must do it *in you*, because God doesn't tend to do *through us* what he hasn't first done *in us*. It's why discipleship precedes mission, and follows it, and precedes it again, and so on and so forth.

Awakening friends, it is all about agency. We are becoming agents of Jesus—becoming like him so we can act in his name, as in, his name is my name too.

Jesus, or Yeshua, is also the name "Joshua." Go figure.

The Prayer

Father, we so readily remember the Bible verse about how you're able to do abundantly above and beyond anything we can ask or even imagine, and we so readily forget how it then says, "according to his power that is at work within us" (Eph. 3:20). We confess, we easily remove ourselves from agency and responsibility. We somehow expect you to just do it yourself, outside of us and other people. Awaken me, Holy Spirit, Christ in me, agency you have created. We get it and yet we don't. We need awakening, Lord Jesus, to your name and in your name, amen.

The Questions

- So from yesterday . . . where is your New Jersey? And, for today, do you see yourself as a bona fide agent of Jesus of Nazareth, the Messiah? Or is that still kind of fuzzy for you?

38 Stop Working for Jesus

JOSHUA 1:7–9 | "Be strong and very courageous. Be careful to obey all the law my servant Moses gave you; do not turn from it to the right or to the left, that you may be successful wherever you go. Keep this Book of the Law always on your lips; meditate on it day and night, so that you may be careful to do everything written in it. Then you will be prosperous and successful. Have I not commanded you? Be strong and courageous. Do not be afraid; do not be discouraged, for the Lord your God will be with you wherever you go."

Consider This

First Thessalonians 5:11 says, "Therefore encourage one another and build each other up, just as in fact you are doing."

I will forever remember my first class of my first day of seminary. It was Asbury Theological Seminary, and the class was Introduction to the New Testament. The professor was Dr. Robert Mulholland. His first words to the class that year (and every other year, as I hear all the time from other classes) were these: "The most important decision you must make in your time at seminary is this one: Will you be in the world for Christ, or will you be in Christ for the world? I am here to help you become the latter."

To be in the world for Jesus implies that I will be doing good things *for* him. To be "in Jesus" for the world, implies that he will be doing God things *through* me. This may seem subtle. It is not. To be "in Christ" for the world means the discipleship journey of becoming a person in Christ. This is the second half of the gospel. The first half of the gospel is Jesus with us and Jesus for us. The second half of the gospel is Jesus in us and Jesus through us.

The story of the Christian faith and the church for the past hundred years is all about Jesus with us and Jesus for us but not so much about Jesus in us and Jesus through us. In response to Jesus being with us and for us, we have done our best to be "for Jesus," which has resulted in an enormous amount of religious activity with very little to show for it.

Notice the progression of God's Word to Joshua so far in chapter 1. Joshua, I am with you. Joshua, I am for you. Therefore, be strong and very courageous. Then note the exhortation toward discipleship—becoming the kind of person in whom and through whom God can live and move and have his being:

"Be careful to obey all the law my servant Moses gave you; do not turn from it to the right or to the left, that you may be successful wherever you go."

It's time to stop trying to do things for Jesus. It's time to become the kind of people in whom Jesus is pleased to dwell and through whom he is delighted to work. It's why Jesus is not looking for employees. He's on the hunt for friends.

The Prayer

Father, this is about an exchange of our old lives for your new life, which is our true selves. We are weary of living out of our own strength. We want to be people who are known by your deep humility and your profound authority and your breathtaking love. Come, Holy Spirit, and lead us deep into the well of becoming like the God who became like me. Thank you, Jesus, for becoming like us so that we could become like you. In your name we pray, amen.

The Questions

- Make sense? In the world for Christ versus in Christ for the world? How would you say it? Highly functioning religious employee versus transcendent agent of Jesus' presence?

39 On Mouthing the Word of God

JOSHUA 1:7–9 | "Be strong and very courageous. Be careful to obey all the law my servant Moses gave you; do not turn from it to the right or to the left, that you may be successful wherever you go. Keep this Book of the Law always on your lips; meditate on it day and night, so that you may be careful to do everything written in it. Then you will be prosperous and successful. Have I not commanded you? Be strong and courageous. Do not be afraid; do not be discouraged, for the LORD your God will be with you wherever you go."

Consider This

Have you noticed how the Bible never leaves behind the fundamentals of the faith? It's right there in plain view again today.

"Keep this Book of the Law always on your lips; meditate on it day and night, so that you may be careful to do everything written in it. Then you will be prosperous and successful."

Translation: Keep your eye on the ball.

I am coming to realize who and what I am in the kingdom of God. I am an awakening coach. I have come to realize this is how many of you see me and relate to me. Either way, I can tell you, this is how I relate to you. I am here to encourage you to get off of the bleachers of passive faith and get onto the field of active awakening. This journey from the bleachers to the field goes by a few different names: *training, conditioning, disciple-making.*

The Christian faith has become more about practicing at practicing, staying stuck in ruts of mindless motions, doing the things of faithfulness without really growing in the strength of faith, and otherwise slowly slipping into a state of sleep. We've got to wake up, people.

I love how the Word of God urges Joshua today to Core Conditioning #1A.

"Keep this Book of the Law always on your lips; meditate on it day and night, so that you may be careful to do everything written in it."

Always. Now here's a fascinating thing about that word. You know what it really means? Always. It means at all times and in all your ways. I am challenged by this.

On your lips. This Book of the Law is the Word of God. It is an audible word. From a quiet whisper to a piercing shout, the Word of God is meant to be mouthed, or spoken aloud. And as it is spoken aloud from your lips, at whatever decibel, it is as though it is coming from the mouth of God—through your lips. Let's remember Isaiah 55. Speak it aloud now:

> As the rain and the snow
>   come down from heaven,
> and do not return to it
>   without watering the earth
> and making it bud and flourish,
>   so that it yields seed for the sower and bread for
>   the eater,
> so is my word that goes out from my mouth:
>   It will not return to me empty,
> but will accomplish what I desire
>   and achieve the purpose for which I sent it. (vv. 10–11)

As the Word of God comes forth from your mouth, it is going forth from God's mouth. It then comes into your hearing. Remember, faith comes by hearing. From your ears it makes its way to your heart and from your heart to your mind, spirit, soul, and strength. It is no accident that the bold admonition to "be strong and very courageous" is immediately followed by the urgent exhortation to anchor down deep into the Word of God. It begins with mouthing.

"Keep this Book of the Law always on your lips."

So will you do it today? Let's just start with the first five words from God—from Joshua 1:7.

"Be strong and very courageous."

All day long I want you to speak these words, aloud, from whisper to shout (you pick based on context). And look for opportunities to speak them to someone else. Remember, they are the words of God and they are powerful and effective. The Word of God accomplishes the work of God . . . every . . . single . . . time.

The Prayer

Father, thank you for your Word. Where would we be without your Word? If we are honest, we can go hours, even days, without it. We are fooling ourselves because we are not really going anywhere without your Word. Would you help us keep this Word of God always on our lips? Come, Holy Spirit, this is who you are and what you do. You cause the Word of God to become flesh, to be like a fire in our bones, to be a lamp to our feet and a light to our path. In Jesus' name, amen.

The Questions

- Do you see how when you speak God's Word it is as though God were speaking it? How does this encourage you? Is your faith rising in the power of God's Word and Spirit? "Be strong and very courageous." How many times can you say this today?

40 Growling in the Word of God

JOSHUA 1:7–9 | "Be strong and very courageous. Be careful to obey all the law my servant Moses gave you; do not turn from it to the right or to the left, that you may be successful wherever you go. Keep this Book of the Law always on your lips; meditate on it day and night, so that you may be careful to do everything written in it. Then you will be prosperous and successful. Have I not commanded you? Be strong and courageous. Do not be afraid; do not be discouraged, for the Lord your God will be with you wherever you go."

Consider This

So yesterday, we delved into "Keep this Book of the Law always on your lips."

And we worked on keeping this Word from God in our mouths all day long:

"Be strong and very courageous."

Anyone who tries this will realize just how challenging it is to keep our attention focused. It is why gentleness (the fruit of the Holy Spirit) is so important. We must not scold ourselves for losing attention or becoming distracted but gently recall our attention to the Word and Spirit.

Now we turn to this next word:

"Meditate on it day and night."

Do you know when that is? Yep. *Always.* It is always either day or night. But this little word—*meditate*—might mean more than you think it does. Many Eastern religions have laid claim to the concept of meditation. The biblical idea of meditation, as I understand it, is quite different. Meditation is often an attempt to empty one's mind. The biblical practice of meditation is about filling one's mind—with the Word of God.

The Hebrew word (transliterated) *hagah* is pronounced "daw-gaw." It means "to growl, utter, speak, or muse." And, yes, you read it right, "to growl." The biblical concept of meditation carries the image of a lion growling over, eating, and savoring its freshly caught prey. We so often think of the Word of God as a duty we must exercise. The Spirit teaches us that the Word of God is a meal to be savored and enjoyed. Recall the signature instruction of Psalm 1: "But whose delight is in the law of the Lord, and who meditates on his law day and night" (v. 2).

I have a working rubric that helps me engage the Word of God over time, and it has led me from a disciplined, dutiful reading of Scripture to a deeply delighted and desirous appetite for God's Word. The hand is the mnemonic device with each finger representing a sequential step of engagement. And, of course, it is alliterated, each beginning with the letter *r*.

Little finger: Read (mouth)
Ring finger: Ruminate (meditate)
Middle finger: Rememberize (slowly load the long-term memory—more on this in day 42)
Index finger: Research (dig deeper)
Thumb: Rehearse (do it)

Ruminate is an agricultural term. It is what cows do when they eat. They delight in grazing on grass. They chew it up. They swallow it and it goes into one of their multiple stomachs where it is formed into a cud. Then they regurgitate it back into their mouth and chew it some more. They are getting every last bit of taste and every last morsel of nutrition. That's how biblical meditation works. We must, however, get to the source—the Scriptures themselves.

In my own personal journey and now significant experience as an awakening and discipleship coach, I find most of us tend to compartmentalize our faith into a small block of time in the mornings. And this time is not so much characterized by reading and ruminating on the Word of God as it is spent reading and thinking about others' thoughts on the Word of God. It's not bad, but it tends to focus on others' words and be short on God's words. Our strength and courage must depend on far deeper sources than the words of women and men. This is why the text makes a beeline from "Be strong and very courageous" to "meditate on [the Word of God] day and night."

"Be strong and very courageous. . . . Keep this Book of the Law always on your lips; meditate on it day and night."

The Prayer

Father, thank you for your Word. One word of your Word is worth more than all of the words of men and women over all the history of the world. How we love your Word and your Spirit. Come, Holy Spirit, and increase our appetite for your Word, our delight in your Word, our desire for your Word. And all of this so that every day we might become made more in the image of your Son, Jesus, in whose name we pray, amen.

The Questions

- Are you more on the duty and discipline side or on the delight and desire side of God's Word? How might you grow more in appetite than aspiration?

The Word of God and *The Comedy of Errors*

41

JOSHUA 1:7–9 | "Be strong and very courageous. Be careful to obey all the law my servant Moses gave you; do not turn from it to the right or to the left, that you may be successful wherever you go. Keep this Book of the Law always on your lips; meditate on it day and night, so that you may be careful to do everything written in it. Then you will be prosperous and successful. Have I not commanded you? Be strong and courageous. Do not be afraid; do not be discouraged, for the LORD your God will be with you wherever you go."

Consider This

My children are turning out to be my best teachers. With each passing day I realize just how much I haven't yet learned. One day, Sam was working on learning a passage of Scripture for one of his classes in school. I noticed him writing it out on a page. He said, "Dad, writing the verse out one time is the equivalent of saying it eleven times." Who knew? I call this practice "scribing," and it's something I try to do with God's Word at least every week. You see, God's Word is a consuming word. It is a totalizing, comprehensive script of absolute wisdom for our whole lives.

"Keep this Book of the Law always on your lips; meditate on it day and night, so that you may be careful to do everything written in it."

Strength in the Lord and the courage to follow him come from depth in his Word and Spirit. Look at the progression here:

1. Keep this Book of the Law always on your lips;
2. Meditate on it day and night; and
3. Be careful to do it.

Most people try to start with number three, fail miserably, and go back to their mediocre comedy-of-errors life. You don't begin with doing it. Frankly, you don't even begin with reading it. You begin with a desire to be strong in the Lord and courageous in following him.

Back to Sam. He had one of the leads in his school play. It was Shakespeare's *The Comedy of Errors.* For three months Sam carried a book around everywhere he went. Yep, it was the script. It was bent out of shape—cover permanently peeled back and pages tattered, underlined, highlighted, dog-eared, and otherwise trashed. I saw that book everywhere—at the foot of his bed in the morning before he woke, in the car on the way to basketball practice, in the waiting room at the orthodontist, on the couch next to the television remote control. You get the point. But here's the kicker. Sam was not memorizing lines. He was learning a character. He was immersing himself in a plot and narrative. He was becoming a player in the story.

He was being careful to do everything written in it.

The Word of God is our script. That's why we call it Script-ure. We are not just memorizing lines. We are learning a character—Jesus. We are immersing ourselves in a plot and narrative. We are becoming players in the story. When we get our eye off of that ball, we so easily slip into a comedy of errors.

So we are beginning to get the picture of rememberize, research, and rehearse, aren't we?

The Prayer

Father, thank you for your Word and for your Spirit who inspired it and who causes it to become living and active in our lives. We want this word to be always on our lips. We want to meditate on it day and night. We want to be careful to do it. But we know that is not really enough. We want to become like Jesus—his character, his mind, his heart, his love. We want to be strong and very courageous like Joshua, Jesus, Sarah, and Mary. Come, Holy Spirit, and usher us deeper into the Script that we might become more and more alive in the unfolding story. In Jesus' name, amen.

The Questions

- What's the story of your own comedy of errors when it comes to the Word of God? Is it legalism? Laziness? Adventures in missing the point? Lackadaisical, lackluster interest? Be strong and very courageous, friends.

42 How to Pass the Test While Failing the Course

JOSHUA 1:7–9 | "Be strong and very courageous. Be careful to obey all the law my servant Moses gave you; do not turn from it to the right or to the left, that you may be successful wherever you go. Keep this Book of the Law always on your lips; meditate on it day and night, so that you may be careful to do everything written in it. Then you will be prosperous and successful. Have I not commanded you? Be strong and courageous. Do not be afraid; do not be discouraged, for the LORD your God will be with you wherever you go."

Consider This

When my oldest son, David, was four or five, we began working on memorizing some short Scripture texts. One day he rounded the corner with great excitement and shouted, "I finally rememberized it!" I corrected, "Oh, great, David, you mean you memorized it." And then I remembered that I was the student in this classroom. He said what he meant, and this has been teaching me ever since. We are well familiar with the rote practice of memorization. Repeat it over and over and over again until you can say it without looking at it. Take the exam and flush. I have memorized so many things over the course of my life and aced so many tests, and I'm sure I got a ton out of it. I just have no idea what. You too? It's a surefire way to pass the test and fail the real course.

So how is rememberizing different? Memorization is the quick loading of the short-term memory. Rememberization is the slow loading of the long-term memory. My grandmother, suffering the worst kind of dementia near the end of her life, could not remember who we were, but she had the Lord's Prayer on demand. She couldn't even remember who she was, but queue up the Apostles' Creed and she was off to the races. Rememberizing comes from the sequence of a way of reading that becomes hearing and mouthing, a way of ruminating that becomes holding and meditating—day after day, week after week, month after month, year after year. Remember Psalm 1 again concerning the one whose delight is in the Word of the Lord and on his Word he meditates day and night. What is that person like? "That person is like a tree planted by streams of water, which yields its fruit in season and whose leaf does not wither—whatever they do prospers" (Ps. 1:3).

This is the real prosperity gospel. See it there in today's text.

"Keep this Book of the Law always on your lips; meditate on it day and night, so that you may be careful to do everything written in it. Then you will be prosperous and successful."

The false prosperity gospel is a transactional formula. If you do this, then God will do that. If you have a certain manifestation of faith or claim the Word of God in a particular way, then God will be bound to grant you the brand of prosperity you desire—namely, worldly wealth and perfect health. It is prosperity on the world's terms. The real prosperity gospel is a transcendent faith. It is about becoming a particular kind of person, a person imbued with divine qualities, who walks in deep humility, profound authority, and breathtaking love, and whose life prospers in surprising and extraordinary ways—even in the most difficult circumstances and losses imaginable. They succeed like a flourishing tree succeeds, not producing but bearing fruit. Their success comes not from a slavish striving after some outcome but from a deep and sustained surrendering to Jesus. In this way of life, this way of delighting oneself in the Lord, we come to desire the life Jesus desires for us. We grow to love in the ways Jesus loves.

And this, my friends, is the real success in life, the success that leaves a long and profound legacy in your wake.

In short, we are going to have to learn a way of approaching God and God's Word that is constitutionally for God and not for ourselves.

"Be strong and very courageous."

The Prayer

Father, thank you that your first words to us were actually a command to flourish. We confess, we don't really understand flourishing. We set our sights so low, and our interests are so self-oriented. I am so weary of the more the world markets and advertises. I want the flourishing of Jesus and his kingdom, the flourishing of trust and rest and love and extraordinary generosity. We are so tired of trying to perfect ourselves for others' approval. We are ready for the flourishing of blessedness in brokenness, of beautiful scars, of the extravagant power of love. Come, Holy Spirit, and sow the Word of God as the script of my life and bring me into the deep character of Jesus, for your glory. In Jesus' name, amen.

The Questions

- Do you know what we call it when human beings posture themselves to try to get God to bless their vision of prosperity and success? Idolatry. Do you know what we call it when human beings posture themselves to receive God's will for success and his ways of flourishing? Worship. How are you making the shift?

43 Presencing the Person of Jesus

JOSHUA 1:7–9 | "Be strong and very courageous. Be careful to obey all the law my servant Moses gave you; do not turn from it to the right or to the left, that you may be successful wherever you go. Keep this Book of the Law always on your lips; meditate on it day and night, so that you may be careful to do everything written in it. Then you will be prosperous and successful. Have I not commanded you? Be strong and courageous. Do not be afraid; do not be discouraged, for the LORD your God will be with you wherever you go."

Consider This

In all these readings and reflections on courage and encouragement, I hope a few things have become evident. First, we are not talking about worldly encouragement. We are talking about the courage of God. Let's remember who is speaking these words to Joshua: "After the death of Moses the servant of the LORD, the LORD said to Joshua son of Nun, Moses' aide" (Josh. 1:1).

All of these words we have gathered around began here: "the LORD said to Joshua."

It is so easy to shift from the main thing to all the things. It is easy to slightly and slowly shift from "the LORD said to Joshua," which is the main thing, to getting our focus

on all the things of studying the Bible and reading, ruminating, and rememberizing and trying to pray more and
then trying to be less busy and hurried, and then someone
says we need to be having a Sabbath day every week, and
then we get convicted about doing justice and caring for
the poor and starting a discipleship band, and before you
know it, we have just traded one set of habits and activities for another set of habits and activities. Then someone
comes along and says we should read Brother Lawrence's
book, *The Practice of the Presence of God*, and it then
becomes less about all those things and more about just
trying to think about God in all the things you are doing all
day long and how this is what "praying without ceasing"
means. It sounds good, but I'm not sure this is true to
Brother Larry's work.

We don't have to throw out all the things, but we must ever
and always be bringing it back to the main thing. So what is
the main thing?

Jesus.

But it's not Jesus as an idea or an ideal or a set of teachings
or miracles or sayings or doctrine or theology or paradigm
or practices or habits or disciplines or T-shirts. Just Jesus.
The beautiful person of Jesus. I'm not talking about Jesus
without the Father and the Spirit, but without Jesus, we
have no idea of the Father or the Spirit. I'm not talking about
New Testament Jesus but Jesus of Nazareth—the Word from
before the beginning of the Bible, who is its inspiration and

author, its fire and fulfillment, and to whom every page points—the Word made flesh. Jesus, our God.

Courage is not the absence of fear, discouragement, or despair. Courage is the presence of Jesus. Jesus is all the courage of God in a human person. The main thing, my friends, is the right here, right now presence of the person of Jesus. It is not so much about practicing the presence. It is about presencing the person of Jesus.

The Lord said to Joshua . . .

What did the Lord say? *"Be strong and very courageous."*

The Prayer

Father, thank you for sending us Jesus, without whom we would have no idea of you. And thank you for sending us the Spirit, who makes Jesus known to us and brings him closer than our breath. How thankful we are to know you. Come, Holy Spirit, and help us to lift our hearts to Jesus, to set our minds on Jesus, to fix our eyes on Jesus, to focus our gaze on Jesus. He is our courage, and to be with him is to be encouraged. Orient all the things into the thing of knowing Jesus, of presencing the person of Jesus—for our good, for others' gain, for your glory. In Jesus' name, amen.

The Questions

- Are you seeing how all the things can get us off of the scent of the person of Jesus? Are you seeing how all the things can be brought into the service of presencing the person of Jesus? How are you seeing that?

Pressing Past the Motions into the Meeting with God

44

EXODUS 33:7–11 | Now Moses used to take a tent and pitch it outside the camp some distance away, calling it the "tent of meeting." Anyone inquiring of the LORD would go to the tent of meeting outside the camp. And whenever Moses went out to the tent, all the people rose and stood at the entrances to their tents, watching Moses until he entered the tent. As Moses went into the tent, the pillar of cloud would come down and stay at the entrance, while the LORD spoke with Moses. Whenever the people saw the pillar of cloud standing at the entrance to the tent, they all stood and worshiped, each at the entrance to their tent. The LORD would speak to Moses face to face, as one speaks to a friend. Then Moses would return to the camp, but his young aide Joshua son of Nun did not leave the tent.

Consider This

But his young aide Joshua son of Nun did not leave the tent.
In those days, I think of Joshua as maybe somewhere between sixteen and twenty. He was Moses' aide-de-camp. Why did Joshua go to the tent of meeting? Because Moses, his leader, went. Why did Moses go to the tent? To meet with God.

The LORD would speak to Moses face to face, as one speaks to a friend.

Why did Joshua not leave the tent when Moses left?

My hunch: Joshua was learning to meet with God, and something tells me the Lord would speak to Joshua face-to-face, as one speaks to a friend. Something tells me Moses actually invited Joshua into his meeting with God, and they shared in this face-to-face encounter with God and each other.

Growing up in the church, it never really occurred to me that going to church was meeting with God. And for the longest time, daily quiet time was not really a meeting with God. It was reading a devotion and saying a prayer (and slipping in and out of sleep if I'm honest). These practices of going to church and daily devotions were my faithfulness to the motions as I had learned them, but I'm afraid these faithful practices missed the movement of God altogether—well-grooved forms of faith but no power of God.

David inspired us: "My soul thirsts for God, for the living God. When can I go and meet with God?" (Ps. 42:2).

Joshua knew God because he met with God, day after day, year after year, face-to-face, as a person speaks with their friend. There comes a point in this journey, if we can stay awake with Jesus and deepen our awareness of his presence, our attention to his words, our attunement to his voice, and our attachment to his heart, that we will find him abiding in us all the time and we in him. Though we leave the tent, the meeting never stops. Moses left the tent, but he never left the meeting with God.

But his young aide Joshua son of Nun did not leave the tent.
Joshua was learning to meet with God.

Years later, when it mattered most, Joshua was able to give encouragement to others because he had the courage of God coursing through him.

Your heart longs for this. It's the life we were made for—presencing the person of Jesus everywhere and all the time.

The Prayer

Father, thank you for inviting us into the tent of meeting. And thank you for showing us that our very bodies are the tent—the place where our meeting with you can go on and on all the time. Teach us this way of abiding, of moving from awareness to attention to attunement to attachment to unceasing fellowship and communion with Jesus. Come, Holy Spirit, and break through the movements and motions and into the deep mystery of abiding in Jesus. In his name we pray, amen.

The Question

• Are you drawn into this way of learning to leave the tent but never leaving the meeting with Jesus? Talk about your own experience with this.

Jesus Sonders

45

JAMES 1:1–4 | James, a servant of God and of the Lord Jesus Christ, To the twelve tribes scattered among the nations: Greetings. Consider it pure joy, my brothers and sisters, whenever you face trials of many kinds, because you know that the testing of your faith produces perseverance. Let perseverance finish its work so that you may be mature and complete, not lacking anything.

Consider This

My youngest daughter, Lily, taught me a new word recently. She's seventeen and brilliantly insightful. She's the professor of empathic wisdom and encouragement on the faculty at Seedbed. The word is *sonder*. Though it is apparently still making its way to the dictionary, it is a real word. And my autocorrect wants to keep changing it to *wonder* (which is a delicious irony as you will soon see).

To sonder means to realize that every single person you come across and encounter is experiencing a life just as complicated, complex, and intricately challenging as yours is.

Jesus sonders.

Jesus has sondered among us, hasn't he? Job losses, sickness, cancer, financial distress, broken marriages, wayward children, besetting addictions, tragic deaths, even suicide—these are the challenges and hardships being endured by some of Jesus' most faithful followers. Imagine the multitudes of people without Jesus navigating these waters.

One of my favorite country songs from years back spoken of love being a house and noting that it was the only house large enough to hold all the pain in the world. To that I would add this: in the house of love, which is the house of God, there is a hard-to-find room where pain finds its purpose. That room is joy.

James, a servant of God and of the Lord Jesus Christ, To the twelve tribes scattered among the nations: Greetings. Consider it pure joy, my brothers and sisters, whenever you face trials of many kinds . . .

How's that for an opening line! To the followers of Jesus scattered all over the world: Hello, I know things are really hard right now. You are struggling mightily with all kinds of difficulties and trials. I have two surprising words to share with you: pure joy.

Why? James begins this way because this is how life is for everyone and because the followers of Jesus have an opportunity to play the long game with pain and become signposts of the slow-rising beauty of redemption. He says "consider it pure joy" because Jesus can and will assign purpose to your pain. He can and will bring transformation into your trial. Don't let those four words—"consider it pure joy"—be lost on you.

. . . because you know that the testing of your faith produces perseverance. Let perseverance finish its work so that you may be mature and complete, not lacking anything.

A word of caution for encouragers. It is not encouraging for people in a painful trial to hear things like "God has a reason for everything," as though he has somehow purposed and designed this suffering for our good. That's not encouraging. It's really just a way we shield ourselves from the insecurity we feel when something bad happens to someone good.

Everything that happens is not God's will, but God has a will in everything that happens.

To encourage someone in the midst of a trial is to greet them with the embrace of Jesus, welcome them into the house of love, and sit with them until they are ready to walk again. And then wander in the wilderness with them until Jesus leads them into the room of joy, where he himself, in his timing, assigns purpose and meaning to the painful trial. It can take years. This is what he does. He doesn't need explainers. He needs people who will sonder and then wander and then wonder but mostly love, love, love. That is the shape and sequence of encouragement.

Sondering is step one. It is the deep disposition of an encourager, moving about daily life knowing every single person we pass is dealing with a complex set of challenges and likely facing some level of pain and often just struggling with every fiber of their being to hold it together. And this is not to mention the people we already know and love. To sonder is to walk about with wonder at the "trials of many kinds" everyone around us is dealing with every day.

Jesus sonders. Thanks, Lily.

The Prayer

Father, thank you for always listening, for hearing our cries of desperation, for loving us. Thank you for sending your Son, Jesus, to sonder among us, to wander alongside us and reinterpret even the worst suffering of all—his own— and thereby to reinterpret our own trials. Oh, Jesus, how we need you and how we need more of you in us so you can be with others in and through us. Come, Holy Spirit, and lead us deeper into this marvelous mystery, for nothing is more encouraging than this. In Jesus' name, amen.

The Questions

- Everything that happens is not God's will, but God has a will in everything that happens. How do you deal with this concept? What is the difference?

This Is a Test

46

JAMES 1:2–4 | Consider it pure joy, my brothers and sisters, whenever you face trials of many kinds, because you know that the testing of your faith produces perseverance. Let perseverance finish its work so that you may be mature and complete, not lacking anything.

Consider This

Here is a true word of encouragement:

The testing of your faith produces perseverance.

I want you to write that down somewhere right now. It is the Word of God for you today and if not today, then possibly tomorrow or the next day. The testing of your faith will come. Jesus never spoke more plainly than when he said, "In this world you will have trouble" (John 16:33a).

There are people in Haiti reading this today and among the Samburu in Kenya and in the city that is a country, Singapore, and in Peoria, Illinois, and Seattle, Washington, and Clovis, New Mexico, and Raleigh, North Carolina, and on we could go. You aren't necessarily in trouble, but you have trouble right now. Let me put it in biblical perspective: you are struggling in the midst of a trial.

This is a *testing of your faith*. Repeat these words aloud, "This is a testing of my faith." Say it again and again until it registers as your reality: "This is a testing of my faith." Be clear, though: Jesus is not testing your faith. The world is testing your faith, or perhaps it is the flesh (our broken proclivity to sin) or Satan himself.

Now, be encouraged. Jesus just reframed your reality. He gave you authority over what the world, the flesh, and Satan intended for evil, and you blessed it into the hands of Jesus, who is already turning it into something for your good, others' gain, and his glory. How do we know this? The Bible tells me so.

The testing of your faith produces perseverance.

This is not the gut-it-out, white-knuckling, never-say-die, don't-give-up kind of perseverance we have become accustomed to. This is the Holy Spirit–empowered perseverance of Jesus Messiah we are into now. It is the oxygen of faith. Notice who is not producing the perseverance—you. Who is producing it? Jesus, with the Spirit, is doing it, and he is producing it through the testing of your faith. Lean into Jesus, and breathe in the Spirit. Don't be afraid. Do not be discouraged. No matter how bad or hard it is, Jesus has you, and you have him—and he has this!

You don't have to try to have more faith or believe more or wonder if this is happening to you because you didn't believe enough or you somehow deserved for it to happen. This is the "world" that Jesus was referring to as the place where we "will have trouble." We must cease being surprised by it. It is predictable. Let's remember now the rest of the guarantee he gives us: "But take heart! I have overcome the world" (John 16:33b).

He has overcome the world to the point that he can bend its brokenness into breathtaking beauty. It can take time, and that's where we will turn tomorrow—to the fascinating meaning behind the translated term *perseverance* and about letting perseverance finish its work.

One more bit before we close out today. Let's recap the text so far:

Consider it pure joy, my brothers and sisters, whenever you face trials of many kinds, because you know that the testing of your faith produces perseverance.

The text states with emphasis what I must put to us in the form of a question: Do you know that the testing of your faith produces perseverance?

The Prayer

Father, thank you for this encouraging word about how you take what is bad and turn it into something good. Thank you that the testing of our faith produces endurance.

Thank you for the faith of your Word to contend that we know this already. We want to know it at another level. Thank you, Jesus, for the sure warning about trouble in this world and even more for the certain truth that you have overcome the world. Come, Holy Spirit, and translate these verities into the depths of our being. We need to know these things beyond knowledge. Train us in this way of engaging our trials, especially the ones eating our lunch right now. In Jesus' name, amen.

The Question

- How does it encourage you that Jesus desires to stir up your faith in the face of this trial—that you don't have to muster it up yourself, that you don't have to white-knuckle your way through?

47 What Doesn't Kill You Makes You Stronger?

JAMES 1:2–4 | Consider it pure joy, my brothers and sisters, whenever you face trials of many kinds, because you know that the testing of your faith produces perseverance. Let perseverance finish its work so that you may be mature and complete, not lacking anything.

Consider This

Recapping yesterday: our faith is being tested by the world, the flesh, and Satan—all the time. We need to restate our words aloud from yesterday: "This is a testing of my faith."

How does this work? Just how does the testing of our faith produce perseverance? The test creates the opportunity for Jesus to transcend and transform our lives. Perseverance does not come from us. It comes from God. I would press through the words *transcend* and *transform* into the word *transfuse*. *Transfusing*—now there's a word I have never used, but I sensed it was the word. I looked it up.

The first definition relates to blood and the obvious connection to a blood transfusion, which itself has interesting implications when it comes to Jesus. The second definition is the bingo: to "cause (something or someone) to be permeated or infused by something."

I don't know about you, but the fireworks are going off for me. To cause to pass from one person to another sounds like Jesus' very words when he said, "Abide in me and I will abide in you."

It gets really interesting when we get to the origins of the word *transfuse*. Check this out:

"Late Middle English (in the sense 'cause to pass from one person to another'): from Latin transfus- 'poured from one container to another', from the verb transfundere, from trans- 'across' + fundere 'pour'."*

---

* Lexico, s.v. "transfuse," accessed November 16, 2021, https://www.lexico.com/en /definition/transfuse.

More fireworks. To pour from one container to another—to pour across—evokes all the imagery of the Holy Spirit being poured out on the Day of Pentecost and thereafter.

Transfusing. This is how the testing of our faith produces perseverance. Jesus causes his life to pass from his person into your person through the pouring out of the Holy Spirit into your spirit.

For the longest time, here's how I thought this process worked: (1) I face a trial, (2) I ask God to help me, (3) I ask people to pray for me, (4) I do my best to get through it, having faith that God is helping me, and (5) I eventually get through it, giving God the glory, thanks, and praise.

In this equation, faith seems to be my belief that God is helping me get through the trial. That doesn't much feel like transfusing, does it? It feels more like God helps those who help themselves. It feels like religious self-help.

Here's the transfusion question: What if Jesus actually wants to come into your core person and take over your life? What if he's looking not so much for "Help me, God" prayers but "Have me, Jesus" prayers? What if Scripture really means it when it says, "I no longer live, but Christ lives in me" (Gal. 2:20)? What if "the testing of your faith produces perseverance" doesn't actually mean "what doesn't kill you makes you stronger"? What if it means the testing of your faith leads to Jesus himself, through the Holy Spirit, persevering in and through your life? What if it means the death of the false self and the resurrection of the true self, which is the transfusion of Jesus into your whole self, body, mind, and spirit? That would be something akin to "pure joy," wouldn't it? That would be indefatigable hope, wouldn't it? That would be breathtaking love, wouldn't it?

This is precisely why our faith needs to be tested, so we can graduate from a spiritualized version of "I think I can" to a meek, poor in spirit "I know I can't" to a sturdy, surrendered, and confident "I know Jesus in me will." The testing of our faith leads us from faith as believing in something to faith as surrendering to someone.

The Prayer

Father, we want to believe this is true, but we have gone so long without really believing it that we wonder if we can make the leap. It is just easier to keep it at arm's length, with you helping us on our terms and us taking it from there. Lord Jesus, we sense you really do want us to belong to you and yet we hold back. We know the testing of our faith produces perseverance, but we need to know it at a whole new level— beyond what we used to think. Come, Holy Spirit, and bring me into a wholehearted surrender, the kind that leads to the transfusing of your life into mine all the time. In Jesus' name, amen.

The Question

- How are you seeing the difference between a transfused perseverance and a gut-it-out kind of perseverance?

48 On Letting Perseverance Finish Its Work

JAMES 1:2–4 | Consider it pure joy, my brothers and sisters, whenever you face trials of many kinds, because you know that the testing of your faith produces perseverance. Let perseverance finish its work so that you may be mature and complete, not lacking anything.

Consider This

Let perseverance finish its work so that you may be mature and complete, not lacking anything.

It is so clear, isn't it? Perseverance is not something we are doing. It is something that is being done within us. Perseverance is what Jesus through his Spirit is doing. To persevere is to participate with the Holy Spirit's work to image us in the image of Jesus. The operative word is *let*. Oh, how we need this kind of holy imagination in the face of a test or trial.

Let perseverance finish its work . . .

Can you "let perseverance finish its work"? In the deepest pit of despair, can you muster the faith to mouth the words, "Jesus, I belong to you"? This trial is happening *to* you, but the work of Jesus is happening *in* you. Don't fight the trial. Lean into Jesus. This trial can break you down. It can break you up. These are the conditions for Jesus to break in and to break through. And look what happens when perseverance finishes its work:

. . . so that you may be mature and complete, not lacking anything.

The Bible word is *teleios*. It actually means "perfect"—not perfect as in flawless and without error but perfect as in flourishing and fullness, and fullness as in the fullness of God. A trial, in the hands of Jesus, becomes the process of becoming empty of all that needed emptying out so that a new and mature and complete fullness can come in its wake.

To the man or woman reading this thinking all is lost—be assured, perseverance is finishing its work in you. Jesus didn't want this awful suffering for your life, but he is making you whole and mature and full—yes, perfect—through the suffering. Let perseverance finish its work.

Be encouraged today. From this trial, though it be a testing of your faith, will come deep humility, profound authority, and breathtaking love. It is already happening.

The Prayer

Father, we especially pray for the one who is thinking of taking their own life today. And we pray for the eyes to see and the ears to hear and the heart to turn to who that may be in our own context—especially the young among us—and love them extravagantly. Lord Jesus, we want to let perseverance finish its work in us. The Bible tells us you were made perfect through what you suffered, and you were already perfect, so we know you did that for us to show us what it looks like. You are the one who perseveres for the joy set before you, and we bless you to persevere in and through us today. Come, Holy

Spirit, and make us mature, complete, and perfect—filled to the measure of all the fullness of God. In Jesus' name, amen.

The Questions

- How is perseverance finishing its work in you right about now? How is that going? What does it feel like? How are you understanding and interpreting it?

49 Show Me the Hoop-om-on-ay'

ROMANS 15:4–6 NASB | For whatever was written in earlier times was written for our instruction, so that through perseverance and the encouragement of the Scriptures we might have hope. Now may the God who gives perseverance and encouragement grant you to be of the same mind with one another, according to Christ Jesus, so that with one purpose and one voice you may glorify the God and Father of our Lord Jesus Christ.

Consider This

Don't you love it when the Bible brings two of our favorite words together twice in two verses? What a sight to behold! And there they are! *Perseverance* and *encouragement*.

They aren't like brothers or sisters or even cousins. They are the same person. The name is Jesus and your name too. This whole series has been about encouragement—and not the thin humanistic notion of giving someone a positive word or a pat on the back. When the Bible says "encouragement," the meaning is thick. This is why the original languages matter so much.

The Bible word for encouragement is pronounced "par-ak'-lay-sis." It means "an intimate call or urging personally given by someone close beside delivering God's verdict." I love that—delivering God's verdict.

Now, if you will humor me, let's remember my (some say) very wordy definition of biblical encouragement.

> To encourage in the biblical sense of the term is to stand in the stead and agency of Jesus, participating in the work of the Holy Spirit, to minister grace to human beings at the level of their inner person, communicating, conveying, and imparting life, love, courage, comfort, consolation, joy, peace, hope, faith, and other dispensations and manifestations of the kingdom of heaven as the moment invites or requires.

When we encourage each other in this sense, we—in the most real and tangible way—become the bearers or agents of God to one another. The agency of God, as revealed in Scripture, is Jesus abiding in us and working by his Spirit through us. In other words, when we encourage in Jesus' name, he is the one in fact doing it, under the auspices of our name.

When we encourage one another in this fashion, it contributes to the catalyzing of perseverance as we have studied it the past few days—that is, "because you know that the testing of your faith produces perseverance. Let perseverance finish its work so that you may be mature and complete, not lacking anything" (James 1:2–4).

Now, the Bible word for *perseverance* is pronounced "hoop-om-on-ay'." It means the presence of God abiding with and transfusing the deep disposition of patient waiting, stead-fastness, endurance, and even joy.

Now may the God who gives perseverance and encouragement . . .

The Prayer

Father, thank you for these words from your Word: *encouragement* and *perseverance*. Reveal the mysteries of their inner workings to us that we might more fully participate with you in this ministry to others. Lord Jesus, would you lead us in a step-by-step way in how we can encourage others? Would you give us your heart and mind for those around us and the boldness to take risks in reaching out to them? Come, Holy Spirit, and bring us the encouragement we need right now and the perseverance of your presence in us. We pray in Jesus' name, amen.

The Question

- Tell a story of how Jesus through his Spirit has encouraged someone through you in recent days.

The Time Habakkuk and James Met Up at the Bottom of the World and Did a Fist Bump

50

ROMANS 15:4–6 NASB | For whatever was written in earlier times was written for our instruction, so that through perseverance and the encouragement of the Scriptures we might have hope. Now may the God who gives perseverance and encouragement grant you to be of the same mind with one another, according to Christ Jesus, so that with one purpose and one voice you may glorify the God and Father of our Lord Jesus Christ.

Consider This

I wonder if you picked up on the little jewel in verse 4 of our text from yesterday and today.

For whatever was written in earlier times was written for our instruction, so that through perseverance and the encouragement of the Scriptures we might have hope.

Speaking of something *written in earlier times . . . for our instruction, so that through perseverance and the encouragement of the Scriptures we might have hope,* meet Habakkuk, a minor prophet prophesying about a major trial on the horizon. I call it "Descent #17."

> Though the fig tree does not bud
> > and there are no grapes on the vines,
> though the olive crop fails
> > and the fields produce no food,
> though there are no sheep in the pen
> > and no cattle in the stalls, (Hab. 3:17)

This is the story of a story not working out like it was supposed to work out and yet working out in a much more surprising way. In other words, it is the story of our lives. It is the story of a baby that will never be born, a spouse who should not have died so soon, a marriage that should not have ended as it did, a career path that just couldn't seem to right itself, an addiction that swallowed up a whole life, a mental illness that led to the brink of bankruptcy and even suicide, and you can take it from here. It is the story of the kind of discouraging situations and conditions that become infected with despair and metastasize into depression and hopelessness. Or worse, it is the more common story of the not-quite crisis—that low-grade fever of a slumbering prosperity without purpose—an illusory life of pain so normalized it has become forgotten, propped up by caffeine and sedated by chardonnay.

Whether screaming or whispering, the song is the same: no figs, no grapes, no olives, no grain, no sheep, no cattle, no energy, no purpose, no light, no life, no happiness, no friends, no lover, no faith, no hope, no love . . . no, no, no.

Into this nothing-doing, nowhere-going existence, Habakkuk deploys lament to lead us to the bankruptcy of the bottom. But look what happens at the no-nothing bottom. Habakkuk and James meet up and do a fist bump. Here's what "Let perseverance finish its work so that you may be mature and complete, not lacking anything" (James 1:4) looks like: "Yet I will rejoice in the LORD, I will be joyful in God my Savior" (Hab. 3:18).

Oh my gosh! Did he really just go there? This, my friends, is a picture of *pure* joy. I used to think that was hyperbole until I realized it was literal. Pure joy is joy untethered from even the slightest shred of happiness. It is inexplicable because it is coming from somewhere other than this valley of the shadow of death and devastation we call "here." It is streaming in live from heaven via the person of Jesus through the power of the Holy Spirit.

To "consider it pure joy . . . whenever you face trials of many kinds," as James instructs, requires faith, because let's be honest, feelings will never get it done in these feckless places. James continues, "Because you know that the testing of your faith produces perseverance" (1:3). This is the stuff of perseverance.

So whether you are at the bottom or you are only practicing for the next trial, I want you to repeat the refrain of what I call "Valley #18" after me: "Yet I will rejoice in the LORD, I will be joyful in God my Savior."

The Prayer

Father, thank you for these words from your Word: *encouragement* and *perseverance*. And thank you for the way they capture what Jesus is always doing with, for, in, through, and all around us. We know Descent #17 and the long and winding way down into the valley of the shadow of discouragement. Some of us know discouragement to the point of despair and depression. Our spirits have given up and are succumbing to this valley as a place of residence. Holy Spirit, empower us to even begin to mouth the words to the song of Valley #18: "Yet I will rejoice in the LORD, I will be joyful in God my Savior." Jesus, we need you to help us, but much more, we need you to have us. We pray in Jesus' name, amen.

The Questions

- Can you remember a Descent #17 in your life? Are you in it right now? Are you learning the song of Valley #18? The struggle is real, isn't it?

51 Descent #17 (Part One)

HABAKKUK 3:17–19 | Though the fig tree does not bud
and there are no grapes on the vines,
though the olive crop fails
and the fields produce no food,
though there are no sheep in the pen
and no cattle in the stalls,
yet I will rejoice in the LORD,
I will be joyful in God my Savior.

The Sovereign Lord is my strength;
>he makes my feet like the feet of a deer,
>he enables me to tread on the heights.

Consider This

It was the summer of 2019, and my life was in free fall in the throes of Descent #17. You may be wondering where this strange nomenclature came from. Every summer for the past several summers, my friend Mark Swayze brings a group of student worship leaders to Nashville for a retreat. He always invites me to spend a couple of hours with them. It has become my practice with this group (and with most others I am with) to ask them to share the Word from God they are presently standing on. It usually evokes an immediate response of "Oh snap! I'm not sure" and then a quick flipping through the pages of Scripture in search of one's life verse.

As the sharing moved around the circle and all the familiar and predictable texts came to the fore of the sharing, it came to Jonah. I will forever remember his text. He closed his eyes as he quietly spoke the words:

Though the fig tree does not bud
>*and there are no grapes on the vines,*
>*though the olive crop fails*
>*and the fields produce no food,*
>*though there are no sheep in the pen*
>*and no cattle in the stalls,*
>*yet I will rejoice in the Lord,*
>*I will be joyful in God my Savior.*

The Sovereign Lord is my strength;
he makes my feet like the feet of a deer,
he enables me to tread on the heights.

Never had anyone brought this text in response to the exercise—and rememberized, no less. As he spoke the words, the Spirit of God began to etch them on my heart. Whatever word I thought I was standing on at the moment, it was clear that Jesus was giving me a new word.

Verse 17 describes the stripping away, hence the designation "Descent #17." On that nondescript summer day, I was nineteen years into a descent approaching its third decade. It began as a slow stripping away of an impressive false self that had been forged over the first thirty-ish years of my life. I built an identity centered on high performance, achievement, and accolades, forged on the fragile scaffolding of how well I did plus what others thought of me. There is a Bible word for such a condition of soul: *slavery*. My entire economy of self-worth was chained to maintaining that false identity. No matter how much good I did (and I did a lot of good), at the core, it was really about myself.

At the tender age of thirty-three—the age Jesus died, I like to remind myself—a cross was planted in my life in a most surprising way. I was recruited into a very prestigious (and thankfully fairly obscure) ministry role for which I did not apply, nor was I qualified for. The unlikely conditions of the cross were set as I walked out of a life where I was loved and could do no wrong into a place where I would be despised and could do no right, a place of jaded jealousy and torturous transformation. It became my decade of detoxing from the nascent narcissism of a performance-based identity.

Think of the gears in your car. Park. Reverse. Neutral. Drive. We must live our lives in drive. We will only understand our lives, however, in reverse. We live by looking forward. We learn by looking back. Jesus took that decade and turned my life from a false-self-actualizing ascent into Descent #17. All the things I relied on to prop me up in my own eyes and the eyes of others were stripped away. As I fought and resisted this testing of my faith, he slowly taught me to let perseverance finish its work so that I might become mature and complete, lacking nothing.

On that summer day in 2019, I happened on a defining word that continues to happen in me today. Thanks, Jonah.

The Prayer

Father, thank you for the stripping way of Descent #17. We confess we would never choose that way. That way had to choose us. That way is Jesus, the one who being in very nature God did not consider equality with God something to be grasped but made himself nothing (Phil. 2:6–7). Thank you, Jesus, for choosing Descent #17 and showing us the royal way of the glorious cross, where everything the world, the flesh, and Satan intends for evil you turn to good. Holy Spirit, help us let perseverance finish its work. Lead us into the rejoicing of Valley #19, not because everything has worked out but simply because of who you are. For your name's sake, Jesus, amen.

The Questions

- What word of God are you standing on today? What word is making its way off of the page and into the lining of your heart?

52 Descent #17 (Part Two)

HABAKKUK 3:17–19 | Though the fig tree does not bud
　and there are no grapes on the vines,
though the olive crop fails
　and the fields produce no food,
though there are no sheep in the pen
　and no cattle in the stalls,
yet I will rejoice in the LORD,
　I will be joyful in God my Savior.

The Sovereign LORD is my strength;
　he makes my feet like the feet of a deer,
　he enables me to tread on the heights.

Consider This

We left off yesterday at the point where I was almost certain I was coming to the bottom of Descent #17 after a full decade of hard, slogging disappointment. Little did I know I was only halfway down the mountain. For context, in my story, the first half of Descent #17 ran from 2000 to 2010. The second half would continue unabated from 2011 to 2020. If you were looking in from the outside and at least a hundred miles away, it would have looked like a glorious ascent was taking place. These years were marked by the founding of Seedbed Publishing, the birth of the New Room Conference, the launch of the Daily Text, and many other exciting developments.

At the same time, in retrospect, I get the feeling there was a backroom meeting in heaven one day where some ambitious middle management junior demon asked Jesus for permission to "sift" me. A series of traumatic occurrences and tragic events began to unfold in my home and family that (to anyone inside a hundred miles) would have appeared like we were hurtling down the mountain out of control. I won't go into it other than to say it turned out to be an eight-year train wreck in slow motion in which I lost everything but my children. It is unhelpful at this point to assign fault or blame other than to say it was clearly a trial and test of satanic origins and outcomes. There is no acrimony, only pain.

Since January 2020, I have found myself on the valley floor wandering around in the ruins of a life that once was, battling despair, grieving losses, picking up pieces, and mostly just putting them back down and wondering, why Jesus, and what for, and what now? I am also with so many of you, affirming aloud, "This is a test of my faith." With everything in me, I am believing that the testing of my faith is producing perseverance. And I'm learning to let perseverance finish its work so that I may be mature and complete, lacking nothing.

So why am I telling you all of this? This is supposed to be about Bible study, right? Well, I want you to know how the Bible is studying me. I want you to know who you are dealing with—a man who has been broken by life yet who believes every word of Scripture and every word he writes concerning it.

All of this brings me to Valley #18. As I wander the arid floor of Valley #18, I am surveying the wondrous cross from a whole new vantage point and trying to fathom how so much breathtaking beauty and splendor could come from such devastating suffering and brokenness. I'm trying to learn the song of Valley #18.

. . . yet I will rejoice in the LORD, I will be joyful in God my Savior.

Earlier this year as I was working to will my mouth to utter these words I struggled to mean, Jesus spoke to me. In the inaudible, impressionistic way he messages me, he said, "You are waiting on things to get better before you rejoice in me, aren't you?" Picture me in stunned silence—the "mind blown" and "hand over face" emojis appearing above me. "Yes, Jesus, you are right. I am waiting on things to get better. I am waiting on my losses to be restored, for my loneliness to be abated, for my circumstances to turn around before I will be ready to rejoice in the Lord."

Then this from Jesus: "This moment you are in right now—this is the moment you will learn to rejoice in me, or you will never learn it at all. Do not miss the meaning of this moment. Do not let this opportunity pass. Do not wait for things to get better. This is the moment of pure joy. Rejoice in the Lord."

I can't claim to be singing it just yet, but I am saying it. I'm finding the pure joy of Valley #18 is rising slowly in my soul but rising nonetheless. Though the minor chords of the lament of Descent #17 continue to claim the melody of this season . . .

yet I will rejoice in the Lord, I will be joyful in God my Savior.

The Prayer

Father, thank you for your long-suffering patience with us, with me. We have settled for—no, we have sought after happiness for too long now. All the while, you have wanted to teach us joy. Thank you for leading us into a descent that threatened to ruin us because you wanted to redeem us. You didn't rescue us out of it, which we may never understand, but bless you because you are redeeming us in and through it. Jesus, thank you for being our constant companion and for coming alongside us in the form of friends and their constant encouragement. Holy Spirit, bring forth our singing voice into a way of rejoicing in the Lord we have not yet known. Teach us the song of Valley #18. In Jesus' name, amen.

The Questions

- Do you identify with this way of waiting on things to get better before rejoicing in the Lord? What keeps you from rejoicing in the Lord right in the midst of the mess of it all? How do you do it in a way that is not forced but real?

53 The Tiniest Most Powerful Pivot Word in the Bible

HABAKKUK 3:17–19 | Though the fig tree does not bud
and there are no grapes on the vines,
though the olive crop fails
and the fields produce no food,
though there are no sheep in the pen
and no cattle in the stalls,
yet I will rejoice in the LORD,
I will be joyful in God my Savior.

The Sovereign LORD is my strength;
he makes my feet like the feet of a deer,
he enables me to tread on the heights.

Consider This

One of the hardest things about Descent #17 is the way we keep thinking it is going to end soon—like maybe after no figs, and then the grapes are gone. Then it comes to no olives, and you think that will be the bottom of it. Next, it's no grain. Surely things will turn around soon. Then it's no sheep. Sometimes when I'm at Costco and see someone with three cases of wine in their shopping cart I think to myself, *They just can't let the grapes go.* Can we be honest? In the midst of

Descent #17, we just want someone to make it stop. We want to escape it. Then it's no cattle.

"Trials of many kinds" can sometimes come in unending waves, especially as we age. The doctor speaks the dreaded C-word, but they think they caught it early and it's not that aggressive. The surgery doesn't get it all. Then the news it has spread into the lymph nodes. Then your spouse falls and breaks their hip. And all this while you are trying to move into assisted living, and they are trying to age you out of your job. And now they want to take your car keys away from you? Who are these people? My peepaw used to say, "Old age is overrated."

Do I need to encourage you to remember the most neglected affirmation of faith that must be most affirmed (out loud) in these times? "This is a test of my faith."

"Because you know that the testing of your faith produces perseverance" (James 1:3).

Then someone in their thirties posing as Aristotle says to you, "This, too, shall pass," and you think to yourself, "Right! Like a kidney stone!" It just doesn't qualify as biblical encouragement. No, we need to know Jesus is bringing the encouragement and the perseverance by the transfusion of the Holy Spirit. We just have to stop trying to escape the trials and learn how to participate in what he is doing—which is to say, "Let perseverance finish its work so that you may be mature and complete, not lacking anything" (James 1:4).

The telltale sign that perseverance is finishing its work is joy. There is a kind of joy that runs alongside the happiness of life's blessings. These are those gifted times and places in life we can truly en-joy. Then there is another kind of joy that begins to stir in the darkest night. It is not born of happy circumstance and good blessings. This is not the joy of enjoyment. There is nowhere to turn for relief, which is why these occasions tend to be fraught with despair and depression. It is in this place that we have the chance to discover one of the tiniest terms in the Bible. It is a pivot word—the tiniest, strongest, little word this side of heaven. You saw it in the text: *yet*.

It is the first word of the song of Valley #18. This little word functions like a pair of binoculars through which we look back up the long, steep climb of Descent #17. No figs. No grapes. No olives. No grain. No sheep. No cattle . . . *yet*.

If we want to stretch this word out to its longest possible and most substantial rendering, we might say "nevertheless." But we can't go around this word. This is the little word of reckoning, or wreckoning to be more true to the reality. *Yet* signifies everything is not fixed or restored or even improving . . . *yet*. What begins as a whisper must become a shout.

For you musicians among us, *yet* moves like the crescendo from pianissimo to fortissimo.

I like to start out whispering the word and then let it grow slowly in volume. At the midway point, I will get out of my chair and begin to walk around the house, saying it louder and louder until I am shouting it. Then I begin to extend my arms and hands upward with each shout. As I did it today, somewhere along the way the *yet* transformed into a *yes!*

So the invitation today, if you find yourself in Descent #17, let the *yet* lead you to the *yes*. Undoubtedly you know someone in the descent right now. If so, begin to say and pray like this on their behalf.

The Prayer

Father, thank you for this guidance, that the way to yes is yet. Jesus, no one shows us this better than you, who in the deepest, darkest Descent #17 ever recorded in human history said, "Yet not my will, but yours be done" (Luke 22:42). Your yet leads us to your yes. We pray for those who find themselves at the end of their rope today, who don't want to go on. We prophesy this little word *yet* into them now. Holy Spirit lead us into this mystery, this place of profound courage, of deepest truth, of invincible and inescapable life. For your name's sake, Jesus, amen.

The Questions

- What keeps you from declaring the *yet*? Are you still waiting on things to get better before you can go there? Are you still looking for the circumstantial blessings in order to rejoice in the Lord? It's hard, isn't it? Can we be honest, even if it is not the answer we would like to have right now?

54 Joy Is the Bonfire of Our Brokenness

HABAKKUK 3:17–19 | Though the fig tree does not bud
   and there are no grapes on the vines,
though the olive crop fails
   and the fields produce no food,
though there are no sheep in the pen
   and no cattle in the stalls,
yet I will rejoice in the LORD,
   I will be joyful in God my Savior.

The Sovereign LORD is my strength;
   he makes my feet like the feet of a deer,
   he enables me to tread on the heights.

Consider This

Yet . . .

Now to the rest of the song of Valley #18:

I will rejoice in the LORD, I will be joyful in God my Savior.

Like most people I know, I find the internet often leads me to read a thousand miles wide and a millimeter deep. Instead of digging deeper wells, I find myself foraging broadly. Both have their strengths and weaknesses I suppose. I find myself reading a lot of people I disagree with a lot, but I remain appreciative of their minds and influence. A few years back, along the path of Descent #17, I read a bit by Chip Conley, who said this:

Suffering – meaning = despair.*

I did some reverse math and came up with this one:

Suffering + meaning = joy.

On the path of Descent #17, we want to know why. What's the reason for all of this suffering? What is God trying to teach me? We can spend years trying to ferret out the meaning of trials, tests, and tribulations.

This past summer, I was listening to a podcast with Jordan Peterson when he said something that stopped me in my tracks. "It seems to me that the purpose of life is to find a mode of being that is so meaningful that the fact that life is suffering is no longer relevant."† The minute I heard it, I knew what he was talking about: joy.

I believe this is the purpose of life and the mode of being Peterson speaks of:

. . . yet I will rejoice in the LORD, I will be joyful in God my Savior.

The song of Valley #18 tells of a purpose of life and a mode of being that is so meaningful that the fact that life is suffering is no longer relevant. It causes me to rethink my reframed equation.

It is not suffering – meaning = despair.

It is not suffering + meaning = joy.

No, it is suffering – joy = despair.

Finally, it is suffering + joy = meaning.

---

* Line Goguen-Hughes, "Despair = Suffering - Meaning," *Mindful*, December 13, 2011, https://www.mindful.org/desapir-suffering-meaning.

† https://medium.com/@riskbeingseenpodcast/notes-on-reality-and-the-sacred -lecture-by-jordan-b-peterson-a94df20f650f.

I want to share a lengthy quote from the late Thomas R. Kelly, who wrote *A Testament of Devotion*, a book profoundly shaping my faith to the present day. Some things you read you never get over. This is that for me.

> The last fruit of holy obedience is the simplicity of the trusting child, the simplicity of the children of God. It is the simplicity which lies beyond complexity. It is the naiveté which is the yonder side of sophistication. It is the beginning of spiritual maturity, which comes after the awkward age of religious busy-ness for the Kingdom of God—yet how many are caught, and arrested in development, within this adolescent development of the soul's growth! The mark of this simplified life is radiant joy. It lives in the Fellowship of the Transfigured Face. Knowing sorrow to the depths it does not agonize and fret and strain, but in serene, unhurried calm it walks in time with the joy and assurance of Eternity. Knowing fully the complexity of men's problems it cuts through to the Love of God and ever cleaves to Him. Like the mercy of Shakespeare, "'tis mightiest in the mightiest.'" But it binds all obedient souls together in the fellowship of humility and simple adoration of Him who is all in all.[*]

Now, go back and read that again, slowly and with feeling this time. That feels like fireworks in my soul. As you can

---

[*] Thomas R. Kelly, *A Testament of Devotion* (New York, NY: Harper & Brothers, 1941).

see, far from shooting fireworks, we are starting to build a fire here in Valley #18. We are laying down the broken limbs of our lives, all the sticks strewn down the mountainside of Descent #17. They have only one useful purpose now: to burn for the glory of God. It will be a glorious bonfire before we are done. Joy is that bonfire of brokenness revealing the blessed beauty of the one on fire but not consumed—Jesus—who became like us so we could become like him.

The Prayer

Father, lead me into the simplicity of the trusting child. So many praying here have had this stolen from them somewhere along the way. Yet you are the one who restores our capacity to trust. We want to come to this place, this way of faith where life is so meaningful that the fact of our suffering becomes strangely irrelevant. Thank you, Jesus, for taking us deep into your heart for us and for the world and for your holy ambition to make us as your heart is for the world. Holy Spirit, bring us to the bonfire of our brokenness that we might revel in joy at the blessed beauty you are making of it. For your name's sake, Jesus, amen.

The Questions

- Are you discovering the joy of Jesus—that mode of being that is so meaningful it renders suffering irrelevant? Would you like to find this kind of joy? It is closer than you may think.

55 Hey! I Know the Will of God for You

HABAKKUK 3:17–19 | Though the fig tree does not bud
and there are no grapes on the vines,
though the olive crop fails
and the fields produce no food,
though there are no sheep in the pen
and no cattle in the stalls,
yet I will rejoice in the Lord,
I will be joyful in God my Savior.

The Sovereign Lord is my strength;
he makes my feet like the feet of a deer,
he enables me to tread on the heights.

Consider This

Yet.

Are you still doing it? You know, "yetting." Are you still "yetting"?

There's something I wanted to point out about our text from Valley #18.

. . . yet I will rejoice in the Lord, I will be joyful in God my Savior.

It is the verbs. They are future tense, which is fine until we realize it is never the future. It is always the present. So the time for rejoicing is always right now and the place for rejoicing is always right here.

I have noticed through my season in Valley #18 that to say "I will rejoice in the Lᴏʀᴅ" is not the same thing as actually rejoicing in the Lord. In the same way, I find it easier to say I will exercise and eat healthy every day than to actually follow through on it. "I will" is a good statement of intention, but intention will not get it done. What is it they say the pavement is made of on the road to hell? Oh yeah, right, good intentions.

So how does intention become action? Intention awakens our will, as in "I will." If intention is to become meaningful action, it must first rise to the level of attention.

Intention. Attention. Action.

Intention so often misses the mark of action because it misses the movement of attention. So is the attention on the action of rejoicing? I have tried so many times to go from the intention (will) to rejoice to the action of rejoicing only to find it rote, unsatisfying, and ultimately unhelpful. No, our attention must be lifted and set upon the subject, verb, and direct object of all joy: Jesus Messiah.

Our attention tends to become deeply attuned to our circumstances: no figs, no grapes, no olives, no grain, no chickens, no ducks, and so on. This is why we get discouraged and give in to despair and become depressed. It's why "yetting" is so important. The *yet* shifts us from the no of our circumstances to the yes of Jesus. Our attention must be lifted into the awareness of God. It makes sense, doesn't it? We are, after all, rejoicing *in* the Lord. Attention shifts our souls from mere thoughts about God to dwelling in the presence of God.

I apologize if I am making this more complex than it may need to be, but we are trying to understand something super deep here. The journey from simplistic to simple usually runs through some complexity.

Intention. Attention. Rejoicing.

"Rejoice always, pray continually, give thanks in all circumstances; for this is God's will for you in Christ Jesus" (1 Thess. 5:16–18).

The Prayer

Father, thank you for the way you reveal things to us we could never figure out. Thank you for your Word and Spirit by which you are always working to reveal your will and your ways. Thank you for Jesus, who so faithfully teaches, trains, interprets, and instructs us. We want to offer you the faculty of our attention today. It is battered and broken. Our attention muscles have atrophied from distraction and anxiety. We didn't intend it. Life has broken us. We need healing Jesus, the kind only you can bring. Holy Spirit, would you begin to heal our attention? My soul magnifies the Lord, and my spirit rejoices in God my Savior. I want this to be true for me always and all the time. For your name's sake, Jesus, amen.

The Questions

- Have you discovered the unsatisfying nature of rotely rejoicing in the Lord, of trying to move from intention to action whilst skipping over the work of honing our attention on Jesus? How is this resonating or not with you?

Approaching Ascent #19 | 56

HABAKKUK 3:17–19 | Though the fig tree does not bud
    and there are no grapes on the vines,
though the olive crop fails
    and the fields produce no food,
though there are no sheep in the pen
    and no cattle in the stalls,
yet I will rejoice in the LORD,
    I will be joyful in God my Savior.

The Sovereign LORD is my strength;
    he makes my feet like the feet of a deer,
    he enables me to tread on the heights.

Consider This

For the past six months or so, I have been daily walking through Psalm 84. It's one of the greatest hits of the whole collection. Through the summer a friend and I texted it back and forth, verse by verse, throughout the day every day. This is the slow-walking way of rememberizing. There is a movement in the Psalm reminiscent of the Habakkuk text we've been engaging. Let's call it "The Baka Descent."

> Blessed are those whose strength is in you,
>> whose hearts are set on pilgrimage.
> As they pass through the Valley of Baka,
>> they make it a place of springs;
>> the autumn rains also cover it with pools.
> They go from strength to strength,
>> till each appears before God in Zion. (Ps. 84:5–7)

The Valley of Baka is also known in the Bible as the Valley of Tears or the Valley of Weeping. Here's the fascinating part: those whose strength is in God make the place of tears and weeping a place of springs. It sounds like Valley #18, doesn't it? *Yet I will rejoice in the LORD.* How does one make the place of tears a place of springs? Even more so, how in a place of weakness and loss does this next bit happen? "They go from strength to strength, till each appears before God in Zion."

The groundbreaking secret comes in Habakkuk 3:19, which we shall call "Ascent #19."

The Sovereign LORD is my strength.

Descent #17: No figs, no grapes, no olives, no grain, no sheep, no cattle, no health, no wealth, no happy times, no fun, no vacations, and so forth design to untether us from all the strengths that were never really strengths to begin with.

Valley #18: *Yet, I will rejoice in the* Lord, *I will be joyful in God my Savior.*

Notice it is a different thing to be joyful *for* God my Savior and to be joyful *in* God my Savior. But watch where this mysterious place of power leads:

Ascent #19: *The Sovereign* Lord *is my strength.*

Notice it doesn't say the Sovereign Lord *gives* me strength. It says he *is* my strength. This the difference between Jesus helping us and Jesus having us. This is the whole point of the whole thing, moving from a place of always trying to get Jesus to help us with our plans and purposes for our lives to allowing Jesus to have us for his plans and purposes. It is the difference between laying down the self of our own making and taking up the life for which we were made.

This is the meaning of the great scriptural saying of all the saints: "The joy of the Lord is your strength" (Neh. 8:10).

When the Sovereign Lord is our strength, we are able to go from strength to strength, indeed even glory to glory, despite the most difficult trials and tribulations along the way—even because of them. This is why we can "consider it pure joy" when we "face trials of many kinds" (James 1:2). This is how we know "the testing of [our] faith produces perseverance" and why we must "let perseverance finish its work so that [we] might become mature and complete, not lacking anything" (James 1:3–4).

In the midst of a trial, I really just want relief. Jesus wants deep reformation and restoration. I want help. He wants healing. I want escape. He wants engagement. I want comfort. He wants the conversion of my deepest self into his deepest likeness.

In short, I want him to give me strength to fight my battles. He insists on he himself becoming me and my strength to fight his battles.

And this is why we must encourage one another daily, as long as it is called "today." We are encouraging one another to let go of our old broken selves and "put on the new self, which is being renewed in knowledge in the image of its Creator" (Col. 3:10).

This is how he makes my feet like the feet of a deer. This is how he enables me to tread on the heights. "Therefore encourage one another and build each other up, just as in fact you are doing" (1 Thess. 5:11).

The Prayer

Father, it is overwhelming to consider just how much higher your ways are than our ways and how much higher your thoughts are than our thoughts. It is astonishing to see how this is so perfectly and profoundly demonstrated in your Son, Jesus. It is why we can say with all our hearts, "I just want to know him better and better every single day." Holy Spirit, lead us from our endless asking for help and relief and comfort and escape to simply letting Jesus Christ, the Son of God, have us, hold us, heal us, and make us his own possession. For your name's sake, Jesus, amen.

The Questions

• Do you find these teachings more encouraging or more challenging? How do they encourage you? How do they challenge you? What are you contemplating deeply in them?

Why the Glass Is Not Half Empty nor Half Full—There Is No Glass

57

HABAKKUK 3:17–19 | Though the fig tree does not bud
and there are no grapes on the vines,
though the olive crop fails
and the fields produce no food,
though there are no sheep in the pen
and no cattle in the stalls,
yet I will rejoice in the LORD,
I will be joyful in God my Savior.

The Sovereign LORD is my strength;
he makes my feet like the feet of a deer,
he enables me to tread on the heights.

Consider This

An e-mail came over the Thanksgiving holiday. The opening line said it all: "Jesus is changing my life."

I asked if he had time and was inclined to tell me more of the story. He wrote:

> The story is long. Your part, I was depressed, tired, stage-4 cancer, chemo, for five years. Getting selfish, self-centered. I started listening to Seedbed a couple of years ago. When I started listening, I started studying. Every night I listen, study, pray, review on my day. My thoughts left me and I started realizing JESUS, start to finish JESUS. I learned from the word we were studying, started praying for everyone, all day. Started living JESUS. I have learned so much but really it is just knowing JESUS through all things. JD, it is so much more and I love you and pray for you. It is so complicated but so simple.

My goodness, friends! This is the miracle: "I started realizing JESUS, start to finish JESUS. . . . Started living JESUS."

It brings me to yet another mind-blowing Bible text, but first, let's get our coordinates. We are catching our breath in the Holy Spirit oxygen-rich environment of Valley #18, learning the way of "yetting," the mystery of joy, and the practice of rejoicing *in* the Lord, and, yes, all of this before anything changes—while still nursing the wounds of Descent #17. This is the gracious work of Valley #18, preparing us for Ascent #19. As we learn to rejoice in the Lord at the bottom, we find a strange shifting of the center of our gravity. We go from all manner of striving after any form of strength we can find (including endlessly asking God to help us) to realizing "The Sovereign LORD is my strength."

For the last several days I have been wanting to roll out this word from Jesus. It comes from my most all-time favorite campsite in the whole Bible: John 15. Okay, it is really more of a five-star resort and spa for me at this point. After walking us through the most plain-spoken miraculous truth ever released about his life being revealed and sourced through our lives, Jesus tells us why he has just told us it all: "I have told you this so that my joy may be in you and that your joy may be complete" (John 15:11).

This brings a whole new dimension to the saying "The joy of the Lord is my strength."

The joy of the Lord is not a silver lining in an otherwise dark cloud. The joy of the Lord is the revolutionary presence of Jesus Christ himself—in us—transcending our mortal bodies with his eternal life, presence, encouragement, perseverance, love, power, and all the possibilities this means. The joy of the Lord is not a "but look on the bright side" approach to life. This is no "glass half full" mentality. With Jesus, there is no glass, only fullness. The joy of the Lord is exactly what the e-mail said: "I started realizing JESUS, start to finish JESUS. . . . Started living JESUS."

. . . *so that my joy may be in you and that your joy may be complete.*

The Prayer

Father, thank you for the joy of heaven and that you haven't reserved it for some future state. Thank you for showing us this fullness of joy right here and right now in the life and presence of your Son, Jesus. Lord Jesus, we want your joy in us so that our joy may be complete. Lead us to this treasured and gifted place of everyday life, and use our trials to make it even more real. Holy Spirit, you are the joy maker, the one who takes the joy of Jesus and overfills our lives. For your name's sake, Jesus, amen.

The Questions

- Where do you see the joy of Jesus in the stories of the Gospels? Where do you see the joy of Jesus in the lives of people you know? Where do you detect it rising in your life?

58 Jesus Is Changing My Life

ACTS 14:21–22 | They preached the gospel in that city and won a large number of disciples. Then they returned to Lystra, Iconium and Antioch, strengthening the disciples and encouraging them to remain true to the faith. "We must go through many hardships to enter the kingdom of God," they said.

Consider This

"We must go through many hardships to enter the kingdom of God," they said.

I think I missed that sentence in my first dozen or so read-ings through the Acts of the Apostles. And still I hardly grasp it.

So who said this? Paul and Barnabas, also known as the son of encouragement. How could we finish an entire series on encouragement and not meet up with Barnie? We see him first in Acts 4: "Joseph, a Levite from Cyprus, whom the apos-tles called Barnabas (which means 'son of encouragement'), sold a field he owned and brought the money and put it at the apostles' feet" (vv. 36–37).

We might also call him a "son of generosity," right? Later, we see Barnabas sent to Antioch and we get this bit:

> News of this reached the church in Jerusalem, and they sent Barnabas to Antioch. When he arrived and saw what the grace of God had done, he was glad and encouraged them all to remain true to the Lord with all their hearts. He was a good man, full of the Holy Spirit and faith, and a great number of people were brought to the Lord. (Acts 11:22–24)

News of what reached the church in Jerusalem? News of the hardships of the followers of Jesus. Whenever the gospel is about to spread, it is met with opposition of all sorts. The opposition comes in the form of "trials of many kinds," to borrow a phrase from James. And these "trials of many kinds" being experienced by many people all around us all the time create the conditions for the kind of encouragement we have discovered over these past sixty days. It brings us to this word from Barnabas:

"We must go through many hardships to enter the kingdom of God."

Anyone out there seen this one on a bumper sticker lately? It seems to be the opposite of the so-called prosperity gospel, doesn't it? While this may not be suitable for framing or for cross-stitched pillow covers, it does offer the perfect and perfecting framework for real faith. No one ever taught me this. Say it aloud:

"We must go through many hardships to enter the kingdom of God."

Why is this? Why must we go through many hardships to enter the kingdom of God? Because this is where the kingdom of God breaks in—places of loss, suffering, hardship, brokenness, and pain. For the followers of Jesus, when you are being broken down, it is a sign that the kingdom of God is breaking in. Hardships are a sign Jesus is about to promote you to the next level of entrustment in the kingdom of God. This is why the ministry of encouragement figures so prominently in the spread of the gospel of the kingdom.

In the kingdom of Jesus, we don't have merit badges; we have grace scars. Imagine those early Christians still telling their stories and showing off their scars around the campfires of heaven. Remember that time Peter was in prison . . . or when Paul was murdered and left for dead . . . or when Mary the Virgin got the "good" news of the miracle baby . . . or when Lazarus died . . . or when Dad got cancer . . . or when our house burned down . . . or when alcohol consumed a decade of your life . . . or the car crash left you paralyzed . . . or . . .

It brings to mind the lyrics of the great hymn of the church "Crown Him with Many Crowns":

> Crown him the Lord of love;
> behold his hands and side,
> rich wounds yet visible above,
> in beauty glorified.*

You know what a rich wound is? It is a grace scar, gleaming with the glory of God. You know the difference between an unhealed wound and a scar of grace? Encouragement. It's why encouragers are always the forerunners of awakening.

The Prayer

Father, thank you that hardship is the doorway into your kingdom. Thank you for the glorious, gleaming scars of Jesus, who is the suffering one and the risen one, the broken one and the healed one, the High King of heaven and the joy of every longing heart. Thank you that Jesus is changing our lives. Thank you for the hardships and trials because we know in your hands they become the holy transformations we never wanted but would never trade. Holy Spirit, you are the great encourager. Fill our hearts with courage and make us to be true encouragers—the forerunners of awakening. For your name's sake, Jesus, amen.

---

* "Crown Him with Many Crowns," Matthew Bridges, 1851. Public domain.

The Questions

- How about your scars? Are they gleaming yet? What about those unhealed wounds? Are you encouraged to get up and get back in the game? Come on!

59 | It's Today Again

HEBREWS 12:1–3 | Therefore, since we are surrounded by such a great cloud of witnesses, let us throw off everything that hinders and the sin that so easily entangles. And let us run with perseverance the race marked out for us, fixing our eyes on Jesus, the pioneer and perfecter of faith. For the joy set before him he endured the cross, scorning its shame, and sat down at the right hand of the throne of God. Consider him who endured such opposition from sinners, so that you will not grow weary and lose heart.

Consider This

"Jesus is changing me." Nothing has encouraged me more throughout this series on encouragement than this opening line of that e-mail. I'm still not over it.

"I started realizing JESUS, start to finish JESUS. . . . Started living JESUS."

It's why I love today's text so much. It holds the secret to everything: *fixing our eyes on Jesus.*

Here's what happens when we fix our eyes on Jesus: *And let us run with* perseverance *the race marked out for us.*

Some people still believe we can't fix our gaze on Jesus until we have thrown off our entangling sin. People, the exact opposite is true. We can't throw off our entangling sin until we fix our eyes on Jesus. When we do this, sin has a way of becoming irrelevant, doesn't it?

He is the pioneer of our faith. His life authored our faith. So we keep our eyes fixed on Jesus by going over his life, gospel by gospel, chapter by chapter, verse by verse, day after day after day. As we learn the Script, our lives will take on his character—the Holy Spirit moving our faith into all manner of surprising, creative improvisations.

He is the perfecter of our faith. "Abide in me," he says, "and I will abide in you." "Consequently, he is able to save to the uttermost those who draw near to God through him, since he always lives to make intercession for them" (Heb. 7:25 ESV). As we fix our eyes on him, he transfuses his life into our life by the power of the Holy Spirit. And he does not barely save us but completely and profoundly—to the uttermost. The perfecter of our faith actually perfects our faith.

I'll tell you what's perfect. It's where this text goes next:

For the joy set before him he endured the cross, scorning its shame, and sat down at the right hand of the throne of God.

Yet I will rejoice in the LORD, I will be joyful in God my Savior. (Hab. 3:18)

I have told you this so that my joy may be in you and that your joy may be complete. (John 15:11)

Therefore, my friends, when it comes to encouragement, let us end as we began. The late, great poet T. S. Eliot famously said it best:

> We shall not cease from exploration
> And the end of all our exploring
> Will be to arrive where we started
> And know the place for the first time.

The Prayer

Lord, high and holy, meek and lowly,
Thou hast brought me to the valley of vision,
where I live in the depths but see Thee in the heights;
hemmed in by mountains of sin I behold Thy glory.
Let me learn by paradox that the way down is the way up,
that to be low is to be high,
that the broken heart is the healed heart,
that the contrite spirit is the rejoicing spirit,
that the repenting soul is the victorious soul,
that to have nothing is to possess all,
that to bear the cross is to wear the crown,
that to give is to receive,
that the valley is the place of vision.
Lord, in the daytime stars can be seen from deepest wells,
and the deeper the wells the brighter Thy stars shine;
let me find Thy light in my darkness,
Thy life in my death,
Thy joy in my sorrow,
Thy grace in my sin,

Thy riches in my poverty,
Thy glory in my valley.*
For your name's sake, Jesus, amen.

The Questions

- How have you been most encouraged through this series? How are you growing as an encourager?

---

* Taken from *The Valley of Vision: A Collection of Puritan Prayers & Devotions*, edited by Arthur Bennett.

THE SOWER'S CREED

Today,
I sow for a great awakening.

Today,
I stake everything on the promise of the Word of God.
I depend entirely on the power of the Holy Spirit.
I have the same mind in me that was in Christ Jesus.
Because Jesus is good news and Jesus is in me,
I am good news.

Today,
I will sow the extravagance of the gospel
everywhere I go and into everyone I meet.

4/23/22

Today,
I will love others as Jesus has loved me.

Today,
I will remember that the tiniest seeds become the
tallest trees; that the seeds of today become the shade
of tomorrow; that the faith of right now becomes
the future of the everlasting kingdom.

Today,
I sow for a great awakening.

Prayer List

2 Chronicles 7:14

Kathleen + Family
Norma ° Cheyanne
Joe Creekmore + Family
Alyssa/Jason + Family
Brittany/Garrett + Family
Naretya & Family

Staff

Jeanette
Heidi
Denise
Deidra
Melinda
Liz

9 781628 249538